SDG'S FOR KIDS: BUILDING A BETTER WORLD TOGETHER!

DR DHEERAJ MEHROTRA

Contents

Preface

Our world is rapidly evolving, bringing new difficulties and obligations. The UN designed the SDGs to ensure a better, fairer, and more sustainable future for all. World leaders, scientists, and campaigners can help achieve these goals, but so can everyone—including youngsters!

SDGs for Kids: Together, Make the World Better! *is a simple, engaging, and interactive book that teaches kids about the 17 Sustainable Development Goals. Stories, exciting activities, and real-world examples encourage kids to make a difference.*

Chapters on SDG help teachers comprehend complex global concerns, such as climate change, decent education, clean water, gender equality, and conserving life on land and underwater. The book keeps these themes simple and relatable rather than bombarding children with statistics.

After reading this book, young readers will consider themselves SDG Heroes who can improve their schools, communities, and homes. Conserving water, planting trees, and being kind will help the world reach the SDGs by 2030.

We believe young people can transform the world. Let's start this fantastic journey together and improve the world one small action at a time!

www.authordheerajmehrotra.com

CHAPTER ONE

INTRODUCTION

What are the Sustainable Development Goals (SDGs)?

The United Nations has established 17 global goals called the Sustainable Development Goals (SDGs). These goals aim to create a more sustainable, equitable, and wealthy society by 2030. These goals address significant global problems, such as the eradication of poverty, the provision of excellent education, the preservation of the environment, the attainment of gender equality, and the promotion of good health and well-being. The Sustainable Development Goals (SDGs) are a global initiative in which governments work together to create a future where people and the earth may prosper.

Mapping the SDGs

Health and Well-being

Poverty Eradication

Gender Equality

Quality Education

Environmental Preservation

Why are the Sustainable Development Goals Important for Children?

Our choices today will directly affect the lives of children, who are the future of our world. When children learn about the Sustainable Development Goals (SDGs), they better understand global issues such as climate change, pollution, and access to education. More significantly, it allows children to be responsible citizens, critical thinkers, and problem-solvers early on.

Children learn about the Sustainable Development Goals (SDGs) to develop empathy and knowledge of the challenges that affect their communities and the world. They also understand that tiny actions may lead to significant changes, motivating people to make deliberate decisions that promote sustainability and equality.

What are some ways that children may help create a better future?

Even tiny activities children make can have a good impact on the world. Here are a few easy ways that youngsters can help out:

Reduce, Reuse, Recycle: Decrease waste and encourage recycling in your everyday life.

Conserve water and energy by turning off the tap and lights when they are not in use.

Plant trees and protect nature: contribute to creating a more environmentally friendly world.

Be Kind and Inclusive: Show support and respect for others and promote equality.

Learn & Share: Teach oneself and others about sustainability.

Teachers can help students become future change-makers by including the Sustainable Development Goals (SDGs) in their lessons. By gaining knowledge and taking action, children can contribute to a brighter, more sustainable future for everyone.

Why SDGs in Schools?

There are various reasons why including the Sustainable Development Goals (SDGs) in school curricula is vital:

Teaching the SDGs helps youngsters see their role in a global society. It promotes global citizenship and accountability by encouraging people to look beyond their surroundings and consider global issues.

Encouraging Critical Thinking and Problem-Solving: The SDGs address challenging issues such as climate change, poverty, and inequality. As students investigate answers to these *urgent issues, understanding these aims helps them acquire critical thinking and problem-solving abilities.*

Understanding the SDGs helps youngsters become sympathetic to people overcoming various difficulties worldwide. It also develops social awareness. It calls attention to social, economic, and environmental disparities and motivates people to be more sympathetic and environmentally responsible.

Learning about the SDGs helps youngsters become responsible citizens. It teaches students that even small deeds, like cutting waste or saving water, can inspire responsibility and agency and help them achieve more major world objectives.

The SDGs solve problems that will define the future, including climate change, sustainable cities, and excellent education. Knowing these objectives helps children be more ready to face and handle these problems as they grow older.

The SDGs include ethics, social studies, economics, and science, among other disciplines. This multidisciplinary approach makes learning more interesting and relevant, enabling pupils to recognise the links among many spheres of knowledge.

Many educational systems seek to produce well-rounded people who favourably impact society. Teaching the SDGs fits these objectives by encouraging ideals like sustainability, equality, and justice.

Promoting teamwork and cooperation will help us meet the SDGs through group effort. Working on projects related to the SDGs will help children understand the value of community involvement, collaboration, and teamwork.

Early exposure to the SDGs helps kids develop a perspective emphasising sustainability and long-term thinking. Making a more fair and sustainable world calls for this kind of thinking.

Many nations have committed to achieving the SDGs by 2030. Teaching young people about these objectives guarantees that the following generation will be aware of them and ready to help them realise them.

Solved Assignments:

1. *What are the Sustainable Development Goals (SDGs)?*
Solution: The SDGs are 17 global goals set by the United Nations to create a sustainable, equitable, and prosperous world by 2030.
   2. *Why were the SDGs created?*
Solution: Address global challenges such as poverty, education, environmental protection, gender equality, and good health.
   3. *How many SDGs are there?*
Solution: There are 17 Sustainable Development Goals.
   4. *What is the target year for achieving the SDGs?*
Solution: The target year is 2030.
   5. *Why are the SDGs important for children?*
Solution: They help children understand global issues and encourage them to be responsible citizens and problem-solvers.
   6. *How do SDGs impact future generations?*
Solution: Decisions made today will affect the lives of future generations by shaping a sustainable and just world.
   7. *What can children learn from SDGs?*
Solution: Children can learn about climate change, pollution, education, equality, and how small actions lead to significant changes.
   8. *How does learning about SDGs help children develop empathy?*
Solution: Children develop awareness and compassion for others' struggles by understanding global challenges.
   9. *What three simple ways can children contribute to a better future?*
Solution: Reduce, reuse, recycle; conserve water and energy; plant trees; and protect nature.
   10. *How can children conserve water and energy?*
Solution: Turn off taps and lights when they are not in use.
   11. *Why is recycling important?*
Solution: Recycling helps reduce waste and protects the environment.
   12. *How does planting trees help the environment?*
Solution: Trees improve air quality, reduce pollution, and help fight climate change.
   13. *What is the importance of being kind and inclusive?*
Solution: It promotes equality and ensures respect and support for everyone.
   14. *What role do teachers play in promoting SDGs?*
Solution: Teachers educate students about sustainability and inspire them to take action.
   15. *How does learning about SDGs help children become problem-solvers?*
Solution: It teaches them to think critically and find solutions to global challenges.

16. What are some global problems that SDGs aim to solve?

Solution: Poverty, hunger, gender inequality, lack of education, and environmental destruction.

17. Which SDG focuses on quality education?

Solution: SDG 4: Quality Education.

18. How does reducing waste contribute to sustainability?

Solution: It minimizes pollution and conserves natural resources.

19. How can children promote gender equality?

Solution: Treat everyone with respect and encourage equal opportunities for all.

20. What is one small action children can take for a big impact?

Solution: Turning off unnecessary lights to save energy.

21. What does 'sustainability' mean?

Solution: Using resources wisely ensures a better future for the planet and its people.

22. Why is good health and well-being an important SDG?

Solution: It ensures access to healthcare, nutritious food, and clean water.

23. What can children do to spread awareness about SDGs?

Solution: Learn and share knowledge with friends, family, and community.

24. How do SDGs help in reducing poverty?

Solution: They promote economic growth, fair wages, and equal opportunities.

25. Why is it important to take action towards achieving SDGs?

Solution: To create a better world for future generations and ensure sustainable development for all.

CHAPTER TWO

THE 17 SDGs – EXPLAINED SIMPLY

The 17 SDGs – Explained Simply for Students

SDG 1:
NO POVERTY
FOOD

1. No Poverty

What it means: End poverty in all its forms everywhere.

For example, students can donate unused clothes, books, or toys to those in need or organize fundraisers for local charities.

Story: A young boy named Arjun starts a small school project to help kids in his village get basic school supplies.

Fun Fact: Over 700 million people worldwide live in extreme poverty.

Activity: Organize a donation drive for clothes, food, or books.

SDG 2:
ZERO HUNGER

2. Zero Hunger

What it means: End hunger, achieve food security, and promote sustainable agriculture.

Example for students: Start a school garden to grow vegetables. Avoid food waste and share excess food with food banks.

Story: Rina and her classmates start a vegetable garden at school to learn about food and share extra produce with those in need.

Fun Fact: One-third of the food produced globally is wasted.

Activity: Create a "no food waste" challenge at home.

SDG 3
Good Health and Well-Being

3. Good Health and Well-Being

What it means: Ensure healthy lives and promote well-being for all ages.

For example, promote mental health awareness through campaigns for students. Organize sports events to encourage physical activity.

Story: Amit's school starts a morning exercise routine and hygiene campaign to keep students fit and healthy.

Fun Fact: Washing hands with soap can reduce illnesses by up to 50%. Activity: Start a daily fitness or mindfulness routine.

SDDC8
QUALITY EDUCATION

4. Quality Education

What it means: Ensure inclusive and equitable quality education for all.

Example for students: Tutor younger students or peers. Donate books to underprivileged schools.

Story: A group of students sets up a free weekend tutoring club for younger kids in their community.

Fun Fact: Education helps reduce poverty and improve health.

Activity: Share a book or teach a younger sibling something new.

SCHOLS
SDG 5:
GENDER EQUALITY
EQUALITY
5
EDUCATION
EDUCATION
LEADERSHIP

5. Gender Equality

What it means: Achieve gender equality and empower all women and girls.

Here are some examples for students: Challenge stereotypes and promote equal opportunities in school activities. Support girls in STEM (science, technology, engineering, and math).

Story: Neha organizes a campaign to encourage equal participation in school activities for boys and girls.

Fun Fact: In some regions, girls are more likely to be out of school than boys.

Activity: Discuss ways to support gender equality at home and in school.

SDG 6:
CLEAN WATER AND SANITATION
WATER
WATER
CLEAN WATER & SANITATION

6. Clean Water and Sanitation

What it means: Ensure access to clean water and sanitation for all.

Example for students: Raise awareness about water conservation. Avoid wasting water at school and home.

Story: Students in a school create a water-saving club, ensuring taps are turned off after use and teaching others about conservation.

Fun Fact: 1 in 3 people worldwide cannot access safe drinking water.

Activity: Conduct a water conservation challenge at home.

SDG 7.
AFFORDABLE AND CLEAN
ENERGY
ENERGY LIGHTS

7. Affordable and Clean Energy

What it means: Ensure access to affordable, reliable, and sustainable energy.

For students, an example is to turn off lights and electronics when they are not in use and advocate for solar panels at school.

Story: A class science project focuses on using solar panels to power school lights and fans.

Fun Fact: Renewable energy sources like wind and solar are becoming cheaper yearly.

Activity: Switch off lights and devices when not in use.

SDG 8
8
Decent Work and
Economic Growth
SCOOL KIDS

8. Decent Work and Economic Growth

What it means: Promote sustained, inclusive, and sustainable economic growth.

Example for students: Support local businesses by buying their products. Learn about fair trade and ethical consumerism.

Story: Raj starts a small craft business in school, teaching friends about entrepreneurship and teamwork.

Fun Fact: Over 60% of the world's workforce is in informal jobs.

Activity: Organize a small fundraising or entrepreneurial activity at school.

SDG 9
INDUSTRY, INNOVATION
AND INFRASTRUCTURE

9. Industry, Innovation, and Infrastructure

What it means: Build resilient infrastructure and foster innovation.

Example for students: Participate in science fairs or coding competitions. Recycle and reuse materials for creative projects.

Story: A robotics club in school builds an automatic hand sanitiser dispenser.

Fun Fact: Bridges, roads, and electricity are key infrastructures for economic growth.

Activity: Think of and sketch an innovative idea that can improve daily life.

SDG 10:
10
REDUCED INEQUALTIES

10. Reduced Inequalities

What it means: Reduce inequality within and among countries.

For example, students can stand against bullying and discrimination by volunteering with organizations supporting marginalized communities.

Story: A classroom introduces a buddy system where older students mentor younger ones.

Fun Fact: The wealthiest 10% of the world's population owns 76% of global wealth.Activity: Start a kindness project where students help each other.

SDG 11:
SUSTAINABLE
CITIES AND COMMUNITIES

11. Sustainable Cities and Communities

What it means: Make cities inclusive, safe, resilient, and sustainable.

Example for students: Organize clean-up drives in your neighbourhood. Advocate for bike lanes or public transport.

Story: A class project focuses on greening their neighbourhood by planting trees.

Fun Fact: Over half of the world's population lives in cities.

Activity: Organize a school cleanup drive. Illustration: Children planting trees in an urban setting.

SDG 12
SDG 12:
RESPONSBLE
AND PRODUCTION
RESPONSIBLE
CONSUMPTION
RECIUCTIE
CONSUMPTION
WASTUCTION

12. Responsible Consumption and Production

What it means: Ensure sustainable consumption and production patterns.

Example for students: Reduce, reuse, and recycle. Avoid single-use plastics and promote eco-friendly products.

Story: Mia and her family adopt a zero-waste lifestyle.

Fun Fact: If everyone lived like the average person in the U.S., we would need five Earths!

Activity: Conduct a waste audit at home or school.

CLIMATE
ACTION
SCHOOLE

13. Climate Action

What it means: Take urgent action to combat climate change.

Example for students: Plant trees, participate in climate strikes, and reduce your carbon footprint by walking or cycling.

Story: Students create posters on saving the environment and reducing carbon footprints.

Fun Fact: The past decade has been the warmest on record.

Activity: Walk or bike to school instead of taking a car.

SDG 14:
LIFE
BEEOWE
WATER

14. Life Below Water

What it means: Conserve and sustainably use oceans, seas, and marine resources.

Example for students: Organize beach clean-ups. Avoid littering and reduce plastic use to protect marine life.

Story: A beach cleanup program is initiated by school children.

Fun Fact: Over 8 million tons of plastic are in the ocean yearly.

Activity: Reduce plastic use by switching to reusable items.

SDD
5
SDG 15:
Life on land

15. Life on Land

What it means: Protect and restore terrestrial ecosystems.

An example for students is to start a composting program at school, learn about endangered species, and advocate for their protection.

Story: A group of friends adopt and take care of a tree.

Fun Fact: Forests cover 31% of Earth's land area.

Activity: Start a "Save the Trees" campaign at school.

PEACE, JUSTICE, AND STRONG INSTITUTIONS

16. Peace, Justice, and Strong Institutions

What it means: Promote peaceful and inclusive societies.

Example for students: Resolve conflicts peacefully. Learn about human rights and advocate for fairness in your community.

Story: A classroom encourages students to resolve conflicts peacefully.

Fun Fact: There are over 70 million displaced people worldwide due to conflicts.

Activity: Create a peace pledge and have students sign it.

SDG 17: PARTNERSHIPS FOR THE GOALS

17. Partnerships for the Goals

What it means: Strengthen global partnerships to achieve the SDGs.

An example for students is collaborating with other schools or organizations on sustainability projects and sharing ideas and resources to make a more significant impact.

Story: Schools from different countries collaborate on sustainability projects online.

Fun Fact: The SDGs are a global effort involving every country.

Activity: Write a letter to a student in another school about making the world a better place.

Solved Assignments:

1. What is the goal of SDG 1 (No Poverty)?

Solution: To eliminate extreme poverty and provide resources for people in need.

2. How did Arjun help children in his village under SDG 1?

Solution: He started a school project to provide essential supplies to needy kids.

3. What percentage of global food production is wasted, as stated in SDG 2?

Solution: One-third of the food produced globally is wasted.

4. What activity can students do to support SDG 2 (Zero Hunger)?

Solution: Create a "no food waste" challenge at home.

5. What does SDG 3 (Good Health and Well-being) promote?

Solution: Encouraging healthy lifestyles and access to medical care.

6. How does washing hands with soap impact health?

Solution: It can reduce illnesses by up to 50%.

7. What initiative did students take for SDG 4 (Quality Education)?

Solution: They set up a weekend tutoring club for younger kids.

8. How does education help reduce poverty?

Solution: By providing knowledge and skills for better job opportunities.

9. What challenges does SDG 5 (Gender Equality) address?

Solution: Ensuring equal opportunities for both boys and girls in education and work.

10. What activity can students do to support gender equality?

Solution: Discuss ways to support equality at home and in school.

11. Why is SDG 6 (Clean Water and Sanitation) important?

Solution: One in three people worldwide cannot access safe drinking water.

12. What is a simple way to save water?

Solution: Turn off taps when not in use.

13. What did students build for SDG 7 (Affordable and Clean Energy)?

Solution: A science project using solar panels to power school lights and fans.

14. Why is clean energy important?

Solution: Renewable energy sources reduce pollution and are becoming cheaper yearly.

15. What business idea did Raj create under SDG 8 (Decent Work and Economic Growth)?

Solution: A small craft business to teach entrepreneurship and teamwork.

16. What does SDG 9 (Industry, Innovation, and Infrastructure) promote?

Solution: Developing modern infrastructure and technology for economic growth.

17. What initiative did a school robotics club take under SDG 9?

Solution: They built an automatic hand sanitiser dispenser.

18. What is SDG 10 (Reduced Inequalities) about?

Solution: Ensuring fairness and opportunities for all people, regardless of background.

19. What activity can students do to reduce inequalities?

Solution: Start a kindness project where students help each other.

20. How does SDG 11 (Sustainable Cities and Communities) impact our future?

Solution: Make cities greener, cleaner, and more livable for future generations.

21. What action can students take to support SDG 12 (Responsible Consumption and Production)?

Solution: Conduct a waste audit at home or school.

22. How can students contribute to SDG 13 (Climate Action)?

Solution: Walk or bike to school instead of taking a car.

23. What problem does SDG 14 (Life Below Water) address?

Solution: Protecting oceans and reducing plastic pollution.

24. What activity did students do to support SDG 15 (Life on Land)?

Solution: They adopted and took care of a tree.

25. What is the focus of SDG 17 (Partnerships for the Goals)?

Solution: Encouraging global collaboration to achieve sustainability goals.

CHAPTER THREE

CALL TO ACTION

Global Goals for a Sustainable Future

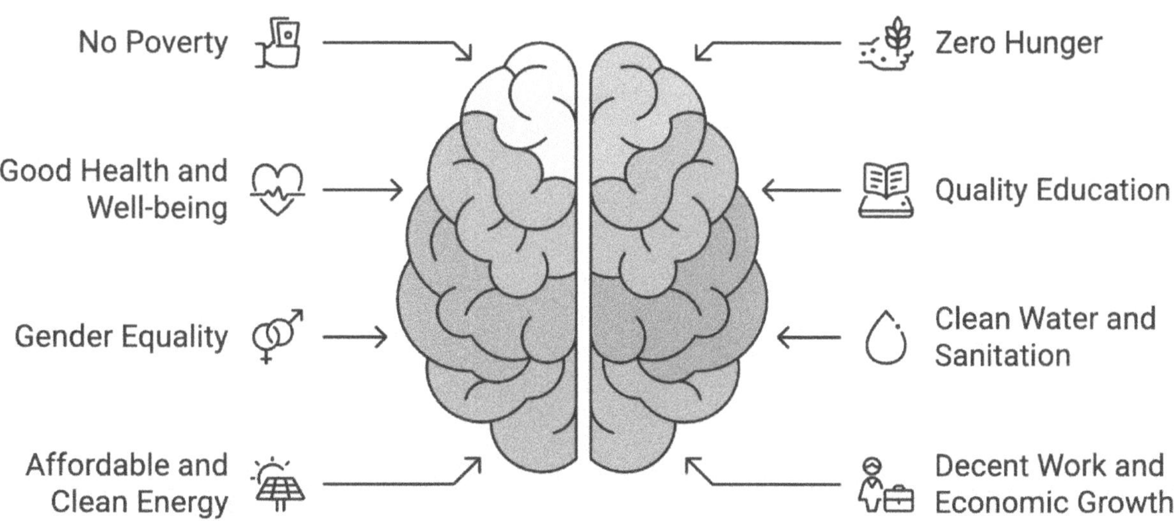

Inspiring Children to Become SDG Heroes!

In what ways might children make minor adjustments in their everyday lives?
Teachers can motivate children to take little but meaningful acts every day to help achieve the Sustainable Development Goals (SDGs).

Here are a few suggestions:

Use reusable bags, bottles, and lunch containers to cut down on trash.

Support your classmates and respect their diversity in order to be nice and inclusive.

Turn off the taps and report any leaks to conserve water.

Make healthy food choices and prevent wasting food in order to eat properly.

You can help out in your town by planting trees or participating in local clean-up events.

Interactive Checklist:

"How many Sustainable Development Goals did you assist with today?"

Teachers can create a daily or weekly checklist for students to keep track of their contributions.

A sample checklist might contain:

* Did I remember turning off the lights I didn't need today? (SDG 7: Clean Energy)
    * Did I offer knowledge or help someone learn something new? (SDG 4: Quality Education)
    * Did I make sure not to waste any food during lunch? (SDG 2: End Hunger)
    * Did I show everyone the same level of respect and fairness? (SDG 5: Gender Equality)
    * Did I choose to walk or ride my bike instead of driving? (SDG 13: Climate Action)

* Did I take part in a community or school service activity? (SDG 11: Sustainable Cities and Communities)

The Role of Teachers:

* Make it enjoyable! Give students "SDG Hero" badges for consistently completing their checklists.

* Promote conversations about the acts that kids took and how those modest efforts lead to a greater goal.

* Set up classroom challenges that allow students to collaborate and innovate in attaining the SDGs.

* By encouraging them to take tiny actions daily, students will learn that every step they take contributes to creating a more sustainable environment.

Teachers play a pivotal role in making Sustainable Development Goals (SDGs) engaging for students. By rewarding children with "SDG Hero" badges, educators can motivate them to take small, meaningful actions toward sustainability. Encouraging open discussions allows students to reflect on their efforts, understand their impact, and connect small changes to larger global goals. Teachers can integrate storytelling, role-playing, and hands-on activities to make learning interactive. By fostering curiosity, responsibility, and teamwork, educators empower students to become active changemakers, shaping a more sustainable and inclusive future for all.

Case Studies about Quality Practices:

Miyagi Prefectural Shiroishi High School, Japan: This school implemented SDG education practices that significantly changed teachers and students. Through various activities, they enhanced awareness and understanding of sustainable development, fostering a culture of sustainability within the school community.

Source: mdpi.com

Global Schools Program: Educators worldwide have successfully incorporated Education for Sustainable Development (ESD) into their lessons and activities. The Global Schools

Program showcases best practices and summarizes lessons learned for educators, school leadership, and policymakers. These case studies highlight creative mechanisms for gaining school buy-in and incorporating SDG activities.

Source: globalschoolsprogram.org

Eco-Schools Program: An international initiative that empowers students to engage in fun, action-oriented, and socially responsible learning. Following a seven-step change process, schools have seen improvements in learning outcomes and environmental impact, leading to recognition with the International Green Flag award.

Source: en.wikipedia.org

These examples illustrate how integrating SDGs into the curriculum can lead to meaningful engagement and positive school outcomes.

Questions & Answers

1. How can children reduce waste in their daily lives?
Solution: Use reusable bags, bottles, and lunch containers.

2. Why is it important to respect diversity among classmates?
Solution: It fosters inclusivity and promotes equality.

3. How can students help conserve water?
Solution: Turn off taps and report leaks.

4. What are some ways to prevent food waste?
Solution: Make healthy food choices and ensure leftovers are not wasted.

5. How can children contribute to their community?
Solution: Plant trees and participate in local clean-up events.

6. What is the purpose of an interactive SDG checklist?
Solution: To help students track their daily or weekly contributions to SDGs.

7. What is an example of an SDG checklist item for clean energy?
Solution: Turning off unnecessary lights (SDG 7: Clean Energy).

8. How does helping someone learn support SDGs?
Solution: It contributes to Quality Education (SDG 4).

9. Why should students avoid wasting food during lunch?
Solution: To support SDG 2: End Hunger and reduce food waste.

10. What SDG does showing respect and fairness to others support?
Solution: SDG 5: Gender Equality.

11. What action can students take for SDG 13 (Climate Action)?
Solution: Choosing to walk or ride a bike instead of driving.

12. How can students support SDG 11 (Sustainable Cities and Communities)?
Solution: By participating in school or community service activities.

13. What is the role of teachers in SDG education?
Solution: To make learning fun and engaging, rewarding students for their contributions.

14. How can teachers motivate students to take SDG actions?
Solution: By giving "SDG Hero" badges for consistent effort.

15. Why are discussions about SDG actions important?
Solution: They help students reflect on their efforts and connect small actions to big goals.

16. What classroom activity can promote SDG teamwork?
Solution: Setting up challenges where students collaborate to achieve SDGs.

17. How does taking daily actions help students?
Solution: It reinforces the idea that small steps contribute to a sustainable environment.

18. What initiative did Miyagi Prefectural Shiroishi High School implement?

Solution: They incorporated SDG education into their curriculum.

19. What was the outcome of SDG education at Miyagi Prefectural Shiroishi High School?

Solution: Enhanced awareness and understanding of sustainable development.

20. What is the Global Schools Program?

Solution: A program that helps educators integrate Education for Sustainable Development (ESD).

21. What is the key benefit of the Global Schools Program?

Solution: It provides best practices for educators and policymakers.

22. What is the Eco-Schools Program?

Solution: An international initiative that promotes sustainability through student engagement.

23. How does the Eco-Schools Program benefit schools?

Solution: It improves learning outcomes and environmental impact.

24. What recognition do schools get in the Eco-Schools Program?

Solution: They receive the International Green Flag award.

25. Why is integrating SDGs into school curriculums important?

Solution: It fosters meaningful engagement and positive educational outcomes.

WAYS TO PRACTICE SDGs IN SCHOOLS

The UN's SDGs address poverty, inequality, climate change, environmental degradation, peace, and justice. By adopting these principles, schools can help students become global citizens and promote sustainability.

1. Curriculum Integration

Include SDGs in all academic lessons.
Make local SDG-focused project-based learning opportunities.
Create SDG-connected multidisciplinary units.
Real-world case studies can demonstrate SDG issues and solutions.
Debates and discussions promote critical thinking on global issues.

2. School Scene

Start school recycling programs.
Create a school garden for biodiversity and nutrition.
Install solar panels in schools.
Give pupils green spaces to study ecosystems.

Conduct energy audits to find improvements.

3. Civic Participation

Work with local groups to promote SDGs.
Clean-up days in communities promote environmental care.
Hold family and community sustainability workshops.
Engage students in local government sustainability issues.
Create an SDG knowledge hub for the community.

4. Empowering Students

Create SDG-focused student clubs.
Inspire students to join worldwide SDG campaigns.
Allow pupils to discuss sustainability.
Hold SDG-focused student conferences.
Develop leadership through service learning.

5. Health and Wellness

Schools should promote mental health awareness and assistance.
School cafeterias should promote healthy eating.
Sports and outdoor activities promote exercise.
Provide stress management and emotional wellness resources.
Teach students about sanitation and clean water.

6. Equality, inclusivity

Awareness programs and workshops promote gender equality.
Provide accessibility for all pupils, including disabled ones.
Celebrate cultural diversity in curricula and events.
Implement anti-bullying activities to make schools safe.
Engage students in decision-making.

7. Green Practices

Schools should reduce single-use plastics.
Start a carpool or bike program to cut carbon emissions.
Use eco-friendly educational supplies and furniture.
Reduce paper waste by encouraging digital submissions.
Hold sustainable fashion and consumerism workshops.

8. Global Citizenship

Teach pupils how global issues affect local areas.
History and social studies should include global viewpoints.
Connect with international schools for cultural exchange.
Encourage language study for intercultural communication.
Promote fair trade in school fundraising.

9. Tech and Innovation

Use technology for SDG research and presentations.
Allow pupils to share sustainability initiatives online.
Environmental coding and robotics projects are encouraged.
Online materials and webinars can teach pupils about SDGs.
Encourage personal sustainability apps.

10. Monitoring/Evaluation

School sustainability goals should be measurable.
Assess student SDG awareness via surveys.
Report sustainability project progress to the community.
Invite students and staff to comment on sustainability.
SDG accomplishments should be celebrated.

11. Career Advancement

Training teachers to include SDGs in their lessons.
Encourage personnel to attend sustainability conferences and workshops.
SDG education professional learning community.
Share SDG teaching best practices with educators.
Encourage teacher collaboration on interdisciplinary projects.

12. Extracurricular Activities

Plan field trips to sustainable farms or environmental organisations.
Hold SDG film screenings and conversations.
Promote environmental competitions and challenges.
Build sustainability awareness through art.
Create an SDG-focused school newspaper or blog.

13. Collaborations and partnerships

Work with universities on sustainability research.
Work with local companies to promote sustainability.
Work with SDG-focused NGOs for educational activities.
Engage parents in sustainability discussions.
Create a school network to share SDG implementation resources and techniques.

14. Advocacy, Awareness

Create SDG awareness programs.
Encourage kids to write sustainability letters to local leaders.
Make school posters and infographics.
Promote SDG-related school initiatives on social media.
Celebrate and educate with "Sustainable Development Goals Day".

15. Financial Knowledge

Introduce pupils to sustainable finance and investment.
Include economic sustainability teachings.
Encourage pupils to create sustainable business plans.

Discuss how consumer choices affect the environment.
Save and budget for sustainability.

16. Research and innovation

Encourage students to study local sustainability.
SDG-focused innovation challenges should be supported.
Recruit sustainability experts as mentors.
Hold environmental and social innovation science fairs.
STEM education should emphasise sustainability.

17. Diversity Celebration

Tell stories about other cultures' sustainability strategies.
Encourage students to share environmental culture.
Celebrate SDG worldwide days.
Create an inclusive, heard-voice environment.
Promote indigenous knowledge and customs.

18. Commitment Over Time

Create a school sustainability policy.
Students and staff should be on a sustainability committee.
Plan a long-term school SDG action plan.
Review and update sustainable goals and practises regularly.
Encourage alumni sustainability involvement.

19. Celebrating Success

Honour student and staff sustainability efforts.
Award exceptional sustainability projects.
Share your successes with others.
Display projects and activities in an annual sustainability fair.

Newsletters and bulletins can promote ongoing activities.

20. Ongoing Education

Update yourself on global sustainability trends.
Encourage pupils to study sustainability.
Provide SDG learning resources for life.
Encourage sustainability curiosity.
Continuously evaluate and enhance sustainability processes.

By applying these methods, schools can promote the Sustainable Development Goals and create knowledgeable, responsible, and involved global citizens.

Questions & Answers

Q1: What are the UN's SDGs?

A: The UN's Sustainable Development Goals address poverty, inequality, climate change, environmental degradation, peace, and justice.

Q2: How can schools integrate SDGs into the curriculum?

A: By including SDGs in academic lessons, creating multidisciplinary units, and using real-world case studies.

Q3: What is an example of project-based learning for SDGs?

A: Local SDG-focused projects where students address community sustainability issues.

Q4: How can schools promote environmental care?

A: By starting recycling programs, creating school gardens, and installing solar panels.

Q5: What role do debates play in SDG education?

A: They promote critical thinking on global issues and solutions.

Q6: How can schools engage students in civic participation?

A: Organizing clean-up days, sustainability workshops, and involving students in local government issues.

Q7: What are SDG-focused student clubs?

A: Clubs focusing on sustainability projects, campaigns, and leadership development.

Q8: How can schools promote health and wellness?

A: By offering mental health resources, healthy cafeteria options, and stress management programs.

Q9: What is an example of promoting equality in schools?

A: Implementing awareness programs and workshops on gender equality and inclusivity.

Q10: How can schools reduce their environmental impact?

A: By reducing single-use plastics, starting carpool programs, and using eco-friendly supplies.

Q11: What is global citizenship education?

A: Teaching students how global issues affect local areas and incorporating global perspectives in history and social studies.

Q12: How can technology support SDG education?

A: Using technology for research, presentations, and online sustainability initiatives.

Q13: Why is monitoring and evaluation necessary for SDG initiatives?

A: To measure progress, assess awareness, and celebrate achievements.

Q14: How can teachers be trained in SDG education?

A: Through professional development, workshops, and collaboration on interdisciplinary projects.

Q15: What are examples of SDG-focused extracurricular activities?

A: Field trips to sustainable farms, SDG film screenings, and environmental competitions.

Q16: How can schools partner with NGOs for SDG education?

A: By collaborating on educational activities and sharing resources.

Q17: What is the purpose of SDG awareness campaigns?

A: To educate students and the community about sustainability and encourage advocacy.

Q18: How can schools teach financial sustainability?

A: Introducing sustainable finance concepts, budgeting, and business planning.

Q19: What is the role of research in SDG education?

A: Encouraging students to study local sustainability issues and participate in innovation challenges.

Q20: How can schools celebrate cultural diversity in sustainability?

A: By sharing stories of sustainability practices from different cultures and celebrating global SDG days.

Q21: What is a long-term commitment to sustainability in schools?

A: Creating a sustainability policy, forming a committee, and regularly updating goals and practices.

Q22: How can schools celebrate sustainability successes?

A: Honouring student and staff efforts, awarding projects, and hosting annual sustainability fairs.

Q23: Why is ongoing education important for sustainability?

A: To stay updated on global trends and continuously improve sustainability practices.

Q24: How can schools involve alumni in sustainability efforts?

A: Encourage alumni to participate in sustainability initiatives and share their expertise.

Q25: What is the ultimate goal of SDG education in schools?

A: To create knowledgeable, responsible, and engaged global citizens who promote sustainability.

CHAPTER FIVE

SUSTAINABLE DEVELOPMENT GOAL (SDG)- ACTIVITIES FOR SCHOOL STUDENTS

Teachers are essential in making the Sustainable Development Goals (SDGs) enjoyable for students. Educators can encourage students to take little but significant steps towards sustainability by rewarding them with "SDG Hero" badges. When students are encouraged to have open talks, they can think about their efforts, grasp the consequences of their actions, and see how tiny improvements can contribute to more significant global goals.

Teachers can make learning more dynamic by incorporating narrative, role-playing, and hands-on activities. Educators encourage children to become engaged changemakers who will help create a more sustainable and inclusive future for everyone by promoting curiosity, responsibility, and teamwork.

SDG 1: No Poverty

No Poverty: End poverty in all its forms everywhere.

Set up a drive to collect clothes, books, and school materials for needy children.

Make banners that talk about poverty and how it affects communities.

Hold a fundraiser to help local groups that are trying to reduce poverty.

SDG 2: Zero Hunger

End hunger, achieve food security and improved nutrition, and promote sustainable agriculture.

Set up a vegetable garden at school and give the food to a nearby food bank.

Set up a food drive to help a food bank or shelter in your area.

Hold a workshop on how to eat in a good and sustainable way.

SDG 3: Good Health and Well-Being:

Ensure healthy lives and promote well-being for all at all ages.

Hold an exercise challenge or sports day for the whole school.

Make campaigns to raise knowledge about mental health and well-being.

Hold a workshop where kids can learn first aid or CPR.

SDG 4: Quality Education

Ensure inclusive and equitable quality education and promote lifelong learning opportunities for all.

Help younger students or your friends who are having trouble with subjects.

Set up a book drive to help schools in places that don't get enough books.

Make movies or podcasts that teach people about sustainability.

SDG 5: Gender Equality:

Gender Equality: Achieve gender equality and empower all women and girls.

Hold a debate or talk about gender roles and fairness.

Please set up a class on women's rights and give them more power.

Start a campaign at school to support giving men and women the same chances.

SDG 6: Clean Water and Sanitation:

Ensure availability and sustainable management of water and sanitation for all.

Hold a water-saving exercise at your school.

Make videos or signs to get people to care about polluting water.

Set up a cleanup effort near areas of water.

SDG 7: Affordable and Clean Energy:

Ensure access to affordable, reliable, sustainable, and modern energy for all.

As a science project, make a small model or gadget that runs on solar power.

Do an energy audit of the school and suggest ways that they can use less energy.

Hold a class on clean energy sources.

SDG 8: Decent Work and Economic Growth:

Promote sustained, inclusive, sustainable economic growth, full and productive employment, and decent work.

Ask business owners in the area to share their stories with the kids.

Hold a career show that focuses on ethical and sustainable jobs.

Make a project about why fair trade is essential.

SDG 9: Industry, Innovation, and Infrastructure:

Build resilient infrastructure, promote inclusive and sustainable industrialization, and foster innovation.

Use recycled items to make a model of a sustainable city.

Hold a game in robotics or innovation to solve problems in the community.

Go to a neighbourhood business to learn about how to be environmentally friendly.

SDG 10: Reduced Inequality:

Reduce inequality within and among countries.
Set up a day for culture exchange to honour differences.

Make a program to get people to understand discrimination better.

Join forces with a school from a different socioeconomic area to do things together.

SDG 11: Sustainable Cities and Communities:

Make cities and human settlements inclusive, safe, resilient, and sustainable.

Making cities and towns more sustainable

Make an eco-friendly plan for your school.

Set up a cleanup drive for the neighbourhood.

Make a model of an urban neighbourhood that can last.

SDG 12: Responsible Consumption and Production:

Ensure sustainable consumption and production patterns.

Get the school to start composting.

Set up a task for "zero-waste" week.

Run a lesson on how to recycle and upcycle things.

SDG 13: Climate Action:

Take urgent action to combat climate change and its impacts.

Take Action on Climate Change

Trees should be planted around the school or in the neighbourhood.

Plan a climate strike or march to raise awareness.

Make a project about how climate change affects your area.

SDG 14: Life Below Water

Life Below Water: Conserve and sustainably use the oceans, seas, and marine resources for sustainable development.
Plan a clean-up of the beach or river.

Make signs to raise awareness about pollution in the ocean.

Hold a film showing how to protect the ocean.

SDG 15: Life on Land

Protect, restore, and promote sustainable use of terrestrial ecosystems, sustainably manage forests, combat desertification, and halt and reverse land degradation and halt biodiversity loss.

Start a garden for wildlife at school.

Plan a wildlife walk to learn about the plants and animals in the area.

Help save species that are in trouble by starting a campaign.

SDG16: Peace, justice, and strong institutions.

Promote peaceful and inclusive societies for sustainable development, provide access to justice for all, and build effective, accountable, and inclusive institutions at all levels.

Run a fake UN meeting to talk about problems that affect people worldwide.

Set up a workshop on how to solve conflicts and make peace.

Come up with a way to stop bullying at school.

SDG 17: Partnerships for the Goals

Strengthen the means of implementation and revitalize the global partnership for sustainable development.

Join forces with another school to work on an SDG project together.

Set up a community event to show off projects connected to the SDGs.

Move social media to get people to know about the SDGs.

These tasks can be adapted to different age groups and school settings. They encourage kids to question things, work together, and take action to make the future more sustainable.

Questions & Answers:

Q1: How can teachers make SDG learning enjoyable for students?

A: Using storytelling, role-playing, hands-on activities, and rewarding students with "SDG Hero" badges.

Q2: What is the purpose of "SDG Hero" badges?

A: To reward students for taking small but significant steps toward sustainability.

Q3: How can students contribute to SDG 1: No Poverty?

A: By organizing a drive to collect clothes, books, and school materials for needy children.

Q4: What activity supports SDG 2: Zero Hunger?

A: Setting up a school vegetable garden and donating produce to a local food bank.

Q5: How can schools promote SDG 3: Good Health and Well-Being?

A: Organizing exercise challenges, mental health campaigns, and first aid workshops.

Q6: What is an example of supporting SDG 4: Quality Education?

A: Helping younger students with their studies or organizing a book drive for under-resourced schools.

Q7: How can schools address SDG 5: Gender Equality?

A: By holding debates on gender roles and organizing workshops on women's empowerment.

Q8: What activity aligns with SDG 6: Clean Water and Sanitation?

A: Conducting a water-saving exercise or organizing a waterway cleanup.

Q9: How can students engage with SDG 7: Affordable and Clean Energy?

A: By creating solar-powered models or conducting an energy audit at school.

Q10: How can SDG 8: Decent Work and Economic Growth be supported?

A: Invite local business owners to share their stories or organize a career fair on ethical jobs.

Q11: How can schools promote SDG 9: Industry, Innovation, and Infrastructure?

A: By building models of sustainable cities using recycled materials or hosting innovation challenges.

Q12: What activity supports SDG 10: Reduced Inequality?

A: Organizing a cultural exchange day or partnering with a school from a different socioeconomic area.

Q13: How can students contribute to SDG 11: Sustainable Cities and Communities?

A: Creating eco-friendly plans for their school or organizing a neighbourhood cleanup.

Q14: What is an example of supporting SDG 12: Responsible Consumption and Production?

A: Start a composting program or host a "zero-waste" week challenge.

Q15: How can schools take action on SDG 13: Climate Action?

A: By planting trees, organizing climate marches, or studying local climate impacts.

Q16: What activity aligns with SDG 14: Life Below Water?

A: Organizing a beach or river cleanup and creating awareness campaigns about ocean pollution.

Q17: How can students support SDG 15: Life on Land?

A: Start a wildlife garden or organize a nature walk to learn about local ecosystems.

Q18: How can SDG 16: Peace, Justice, and Strong Institutions be promoted?

A: Hosting a mock UN meeting or organizing a workshop on conflict resolution.

Q19: How can schools support SDG 17: Partnerships for the Goals?

A: Collaborating with another school on an SDG project or hosting a community event showcasing SDG initiatives.

Q20: Why is storytelling effective in teaching SDGs?

A: It makes learning dynamic and helps students connect emotionally with global issues.

Q21: How can role-playing help students understand SDGs?

A: It allows students to experience real-world scenarios and think critically about solutions.

Q22: What is the benefit of hands-on activities in SDG education?

A: They encourage active participation and help students see the impact of their actions.

Q23: How can schools encourage teamwork for SDGs?

A: By organizing group projects, debates, and collaborative campaigns.

Q24: What is the role of curiosity in SDG education?

A: It motivates students to explore global issues and develop innovative solutions.

Q25: How can schools measure the impact of their SDG initiatives?

A: Track participation, collect feedback, and celebrate achievements through events like sustainability fairs.

CHAPTER SIX

SGD REPORT CARDS

School SDG Report Cards: Why They Matter?

Students learn real-world skills and establish global sustainability responsibility through SDG report cards. Students learn about global concerns including poverty, climate change, and gender equality by tracking their SDG awareness and activities. These report cards encourage kids to take charge, practise sustainability, and evaluate their work. Assessment promotes accountability, leadership, and social responsibility, turning young people become global citizens dedicated to a better future.

Schools grade and give students SDG report cards based on how well they understand and work to achieve the Sustainable Development Goals (SDGs). This is like giving them a "report card" on how well they contribute to global sustainability issues like ending poverty, taking action on climate change, and promoting gender equality through their actions and learning at school.

Important things to know about SDG report cards:

The goal is to raise students' awareness of the SDGs, encourage them to think critically about global problems and inspire them to make sustainable choices in their daily lives.

Criteria for evaluation:

Knowing the different SDGs and how they apply to their community is essential.

Action: Participating in SDG-related school projects, such as recycling drives, community service projects, and campaigns, to raise environmental awareness.

Leadership: Going the extra mile to encourage others to use environmentally friendly methods.

Good things:

Empowerment: Students believe they have the power to make the world a better place.

Holistic learning: ties together ideas about sustainability from different topics, which promotes learning across disciplines.

Community engagement: Encourages working with nearby groups and projects linked to the SDGs.

Problems with implementation:

Setting up clear metrics: Figuring out the best way to measure how much students contribute to solving complex world problems.

Training for teachers: Giving teachers the necessary information and skills to include SDGs in their lessons.

Collecting data includes tracking what students do and how they participate in SDG-related projects.

Parts of an example SDG report card:

Goal-based sections: Each SDG could have its section on the report card where students are tested on what they learn and what they do to support it.

Self-reflection: Students may be asked to think about their actions to help reach the SDGs.

Using peer feedback on group projects tied to the SDGs is an example of peer evaluation.

CHAPTER SEVEN

SDG Success Stories

In order to create creativity, accountability, and leadership in the field of sustainability, it is important to encourage students to think large, perform creatively, and share their journey. Their ability to confront issues in the real world, make decisions that have an impact, and inspire others is enhanced as a result. They cultivate a feeling of purpose and drive forward progress towards a more equitable and environmentally friendly future by becoming heroes of change.

Source: https://www.instagram.com/kolibri_education/p/DF-Ps9KIBKR/?img_index=1

Case Studies:

Source: https://sdgs.un.org/partnerships/sdgs-school
   Success Stories:
1. SDGs Walk (Global Goals)
Mr. Anish Bhurtyl, the first batch of SDGs School graduates, leads this initiative. He just completed his secondary education at St. Xavier College. He has already organized the SDGs Walk in Dhulikhel, Lalitpur, and Budhanilkantha. Now, he plans to visit more than seven destinations.

Detail about SDGs WALK:
SDGs Walk is a bachelor-level youth event that aims to spread awareness of the SDGs. It is primarily based on simplifying

the massive agendas of different sustainable goals and familiarizing people with them.

The SDGs Walk is designed to grab the public's attention and share information about the SDGs. It is scheduled to be organized as an information stall. For every 17 SDG goals, 17 youths will appear, wearing printed caps and T-shirts. The 17 SDGians get together in a familiar place where people flow in the surroundings (e.g., Basantapur, Durbar Sqr., Thamel). They line up in chairs and desks and start interacting with each other. At the same time, they begin the SDG musical performance. They also explain the SDGs needed to understand the performance.

2. HerPad- SDGs Goal no.3: Good health and well-being

Ms Promish Mishra, Mr Sagar Paudel, and Ms Samjhana Shah, 3rd batch SDGs School graduate, led this initiation. The primary objective of HerPad is to provide training to make reusable pad making and menstrual hygiene. Initially, the team offered reusable pad-making training to the women of Central Jail, Kathmandu. After completing the first training, the team was again called to the jail to provide training similar to the next group's. For more information about Herpad, please go through this link: https://www.facebook.com/herpadteam/

3. It's my first period- SDGs Goal no. 3: Good health and well-being

Ms. Dipisha Bhujel, a 4th batch SDGs School graduate, has led this initiation. She is currently taking the MBBS preparation course. She has individually led her action plan: "It's my first period". It's My First Period aims to share information, knowledge, and stories about menstruation and hygiene. She initiated this work through Facebook. For more information, please go to this link: https://www.facebook.com/Its-My-First-Period229196844345989/

CHAPTER EIGHT

SDG Activities in Schools

How Schools Can Incorporate the SDGs:

Curriculum Integration:

Teach students about the SDGs through lessons, projects, and discussions.

School Initiatives:

Start eco-clubs, recycling programs, or community service projects.

Awareness Campaigns:

Organize events like SDG-themed weeks, poster competitions, or guest lectures.

Student Leadership:

Encourage students to lead SDG-related activities and initiatives.

Students can become responsible global citizens and contribute to a better future by understanding and acting on the SDGs!

The following are some measures to relate:

1. Curriculum Integration

Include SDGs in lessons (e.g., science, social studies).

Create multidisciplinary units (e.g., climate change in geography and math).

Use real-world case studies.

Organize debates and discussions on global issues.

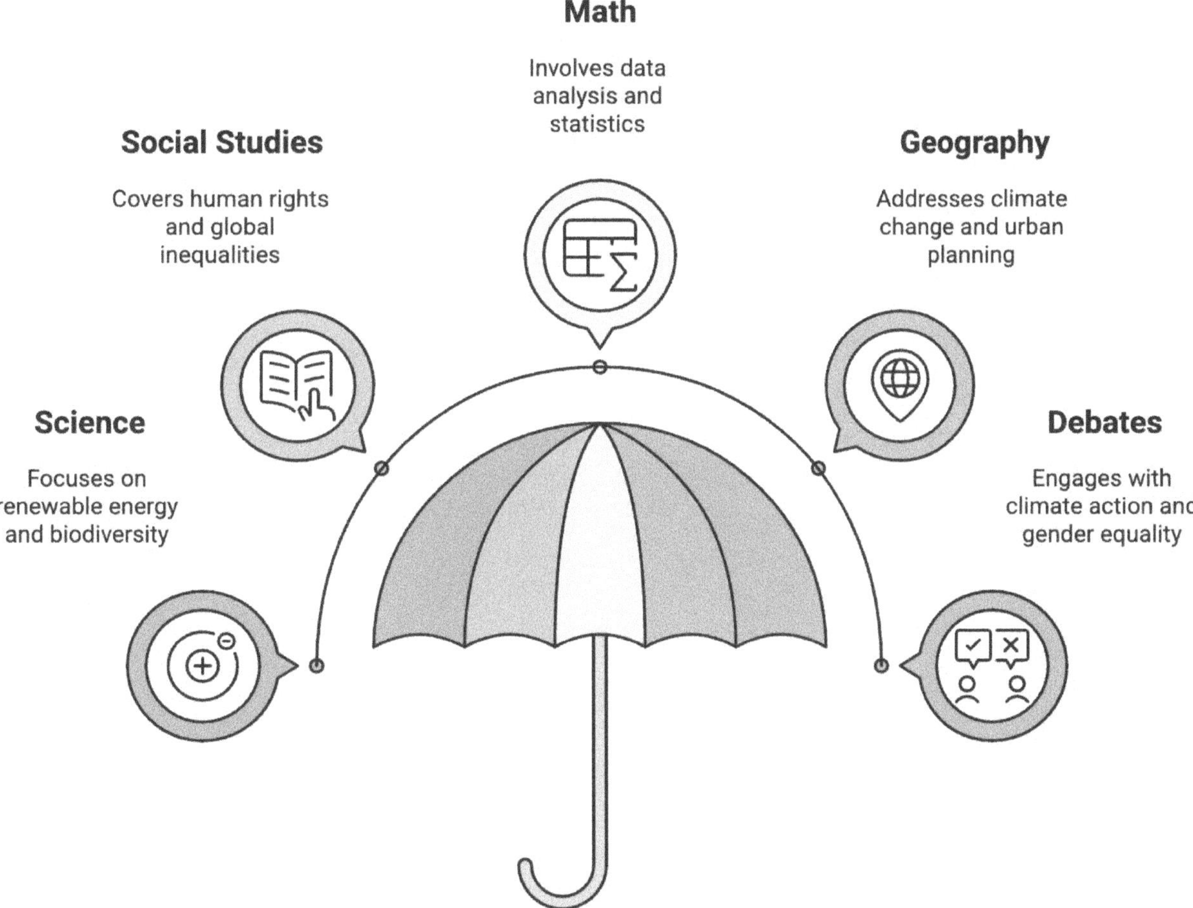

Curriculum Integration with SDGs
Math
Involves data analysis and statistics
Social Studies
Covers human rights and global inequalities
Geography
Addresses climate change and urban planning
Science
Focuses on renewable energy and biodiversity
Debates
Engages with climate action and gender equality

2. School Environment

Start recycling programs.

Build school gardens for biodiversity.

Install solar panels.

Conduct energy audits.

Create green spaces for ecosystem studies.

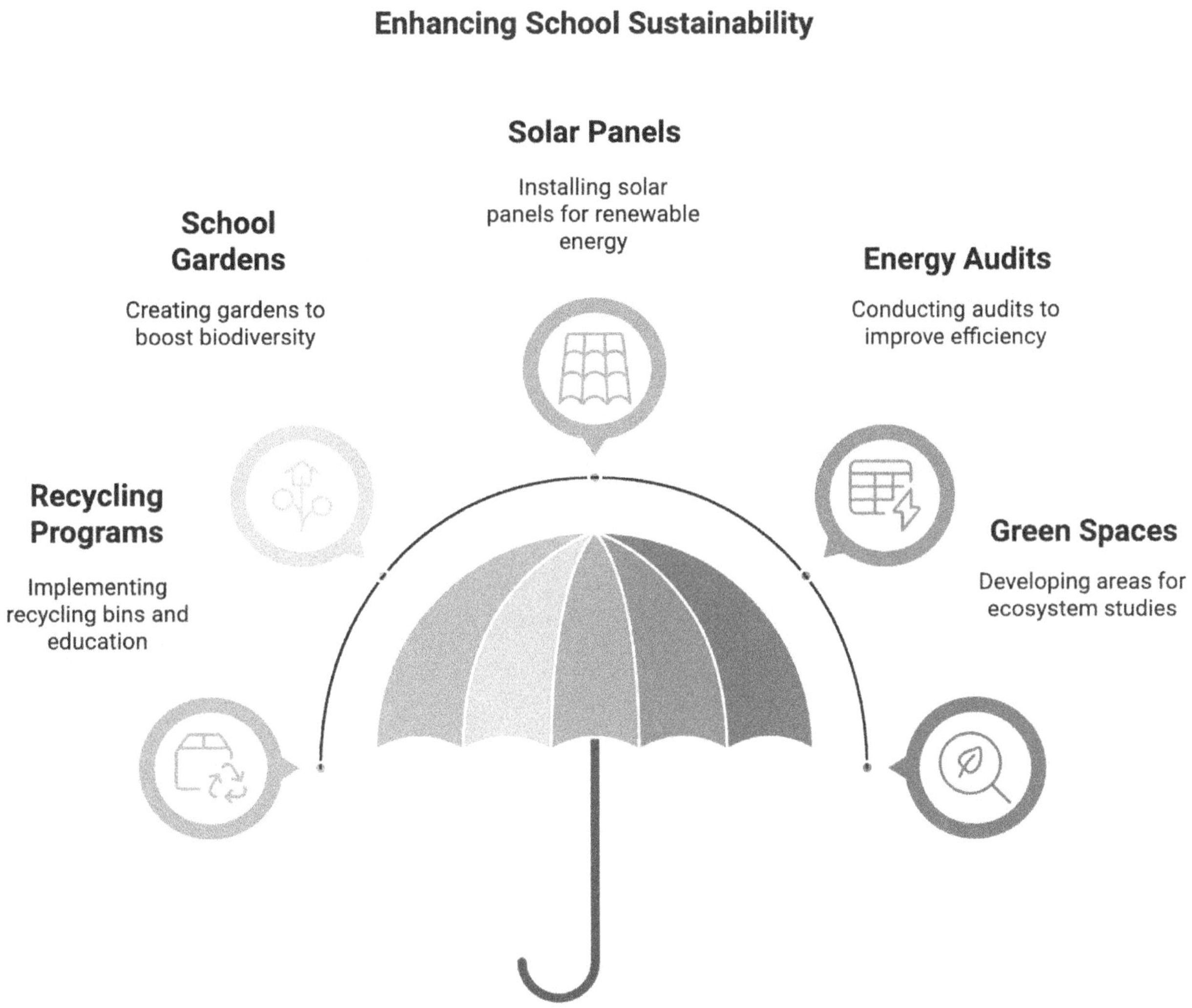

Enhancing School Sustainability
Solar Panels
Installing solar panels for renewable energy
School Gardens
Creating gardens to boost biodiversity
Energy Audits
Conducting audits to improve efficiency
Recycling Programs
Implementing recycling bins and education
Green Spaces
Developing areas for ecosystem studies

3. Civic Engagement

Partner with local organizations.

Organize community clean-up days.

Host sustainability workshops for families.

Involve students in local government projects.

Create an SDG knowledge hub for the community.

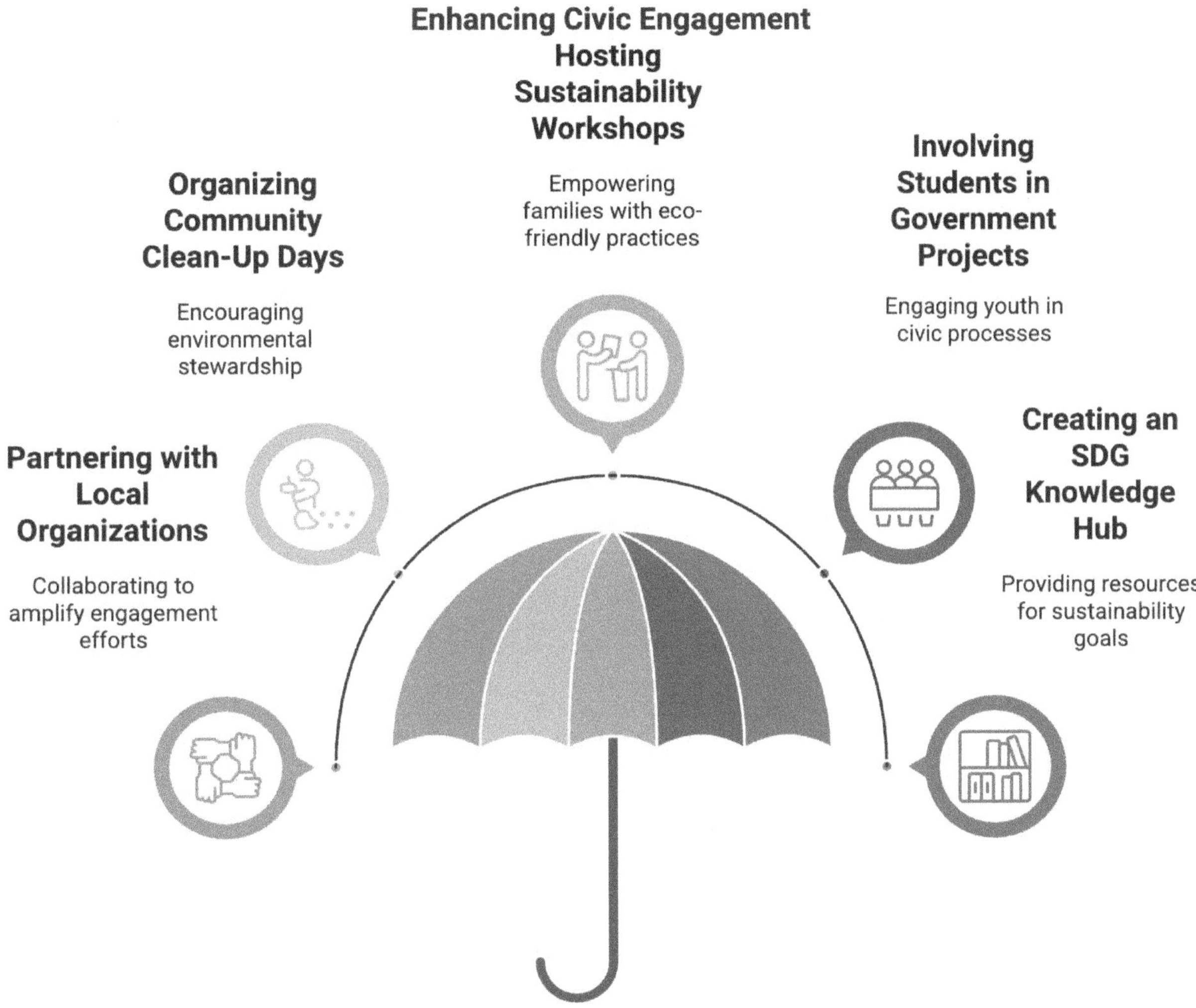
Enhancing Civic Engagement
Hosting Sustainability Workshops
Empowering families with eco-friendly practices
Organizing Community Clean-Up Days
Encouraging environmental stewardship
Involving Students in Government Projects
Engaging youth in civic processes
Partnering with Local Organizations
Collaborating to amplify engagement efforts
Creating an SDG Knowledge Hub
Providing resources for sustainability goals

4. Student Empowerment

Form SDG-focused clubs.

Encourage participation in global campaigns.

Organize student-led conferences.

Promote leadership through service learning.

Allow students to voice sustainability ideas.

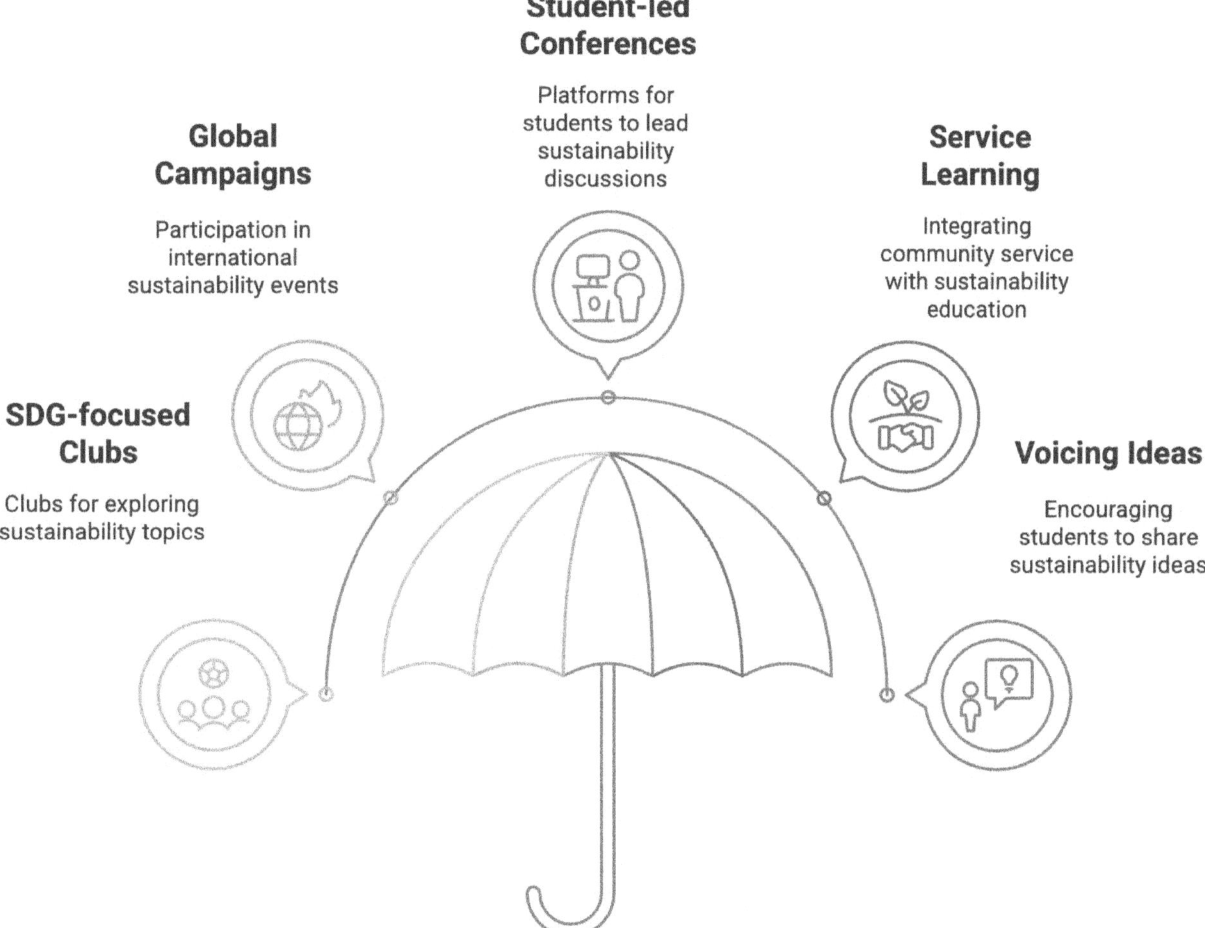
Empowering Students in Sustainability
Student-led Conferences
Platforms for students to lead sustainability discussions
Global Campaigns
Participation in international sustainability events
Service Learning
Integrating community service with sustainability education
SDG-focused Clubs
Clubs for exploring sustainability topics
Voicing Ideas
Encouraging students to share sustainability ideas

5. Health and Wellness

Promote mental health awareness.

Offer healthy cafeteria options.

Organize sports and outdoor activities.

Provide stress management resources.

Teach about clean water and sanitation.

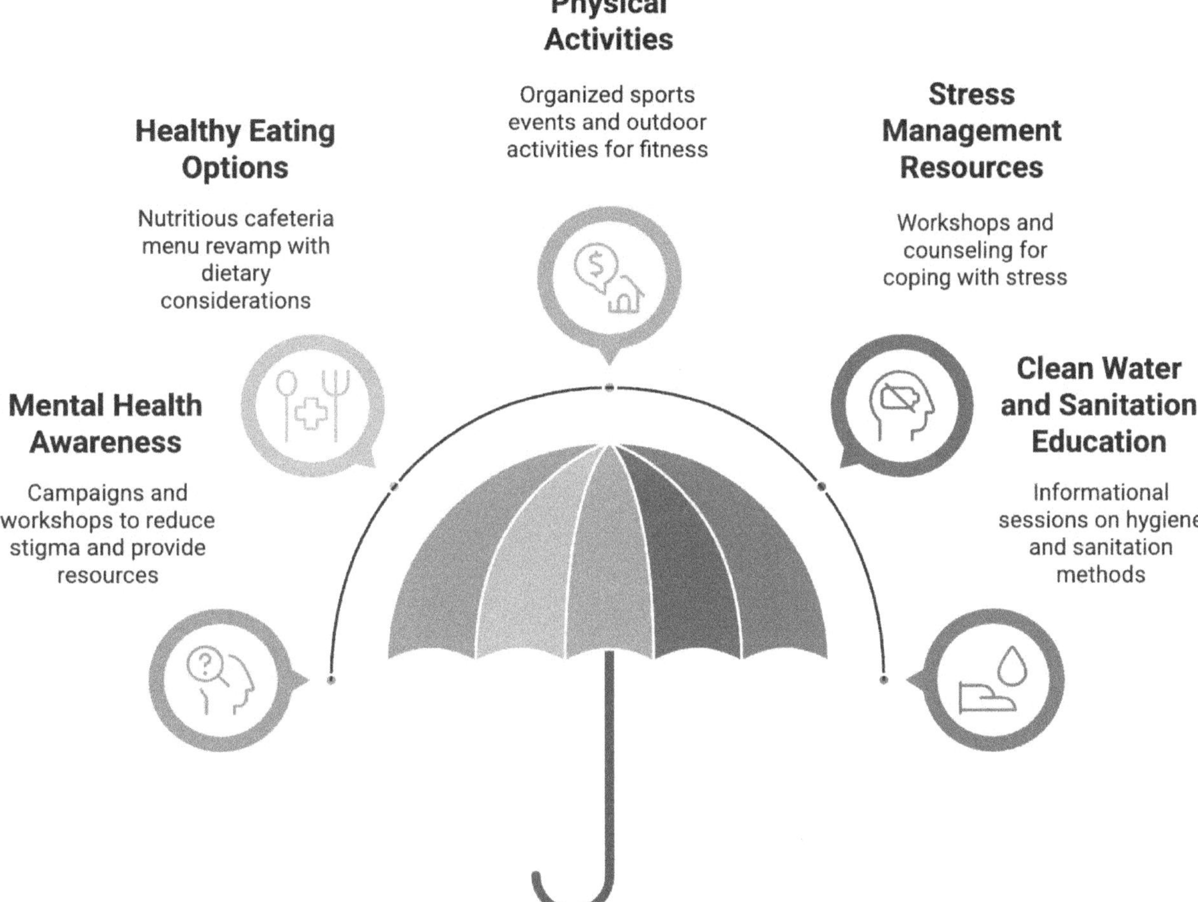

Community Health and Wellness Overview
Physical Activities
Organized sports events and outdoor activities for fitness
Stress Management Resources
Workshops and counseling for coping with stress
Healthy Eating Options
Nutritious cafeteria menu revamp with dietary considerations
Clean Water and Sanitation Education
Informational sessions on hygiene and sanitation methods
Mental Health Awareness
Campaigns and workshops to reduce stigma and provide resources

6. Equality and Inclusivity

Host gender equality workshops.

Ensure accessibility for all students.

Celebrate cultural diversity.

Implement anti-bullying programs.

Involve students in decision-making.

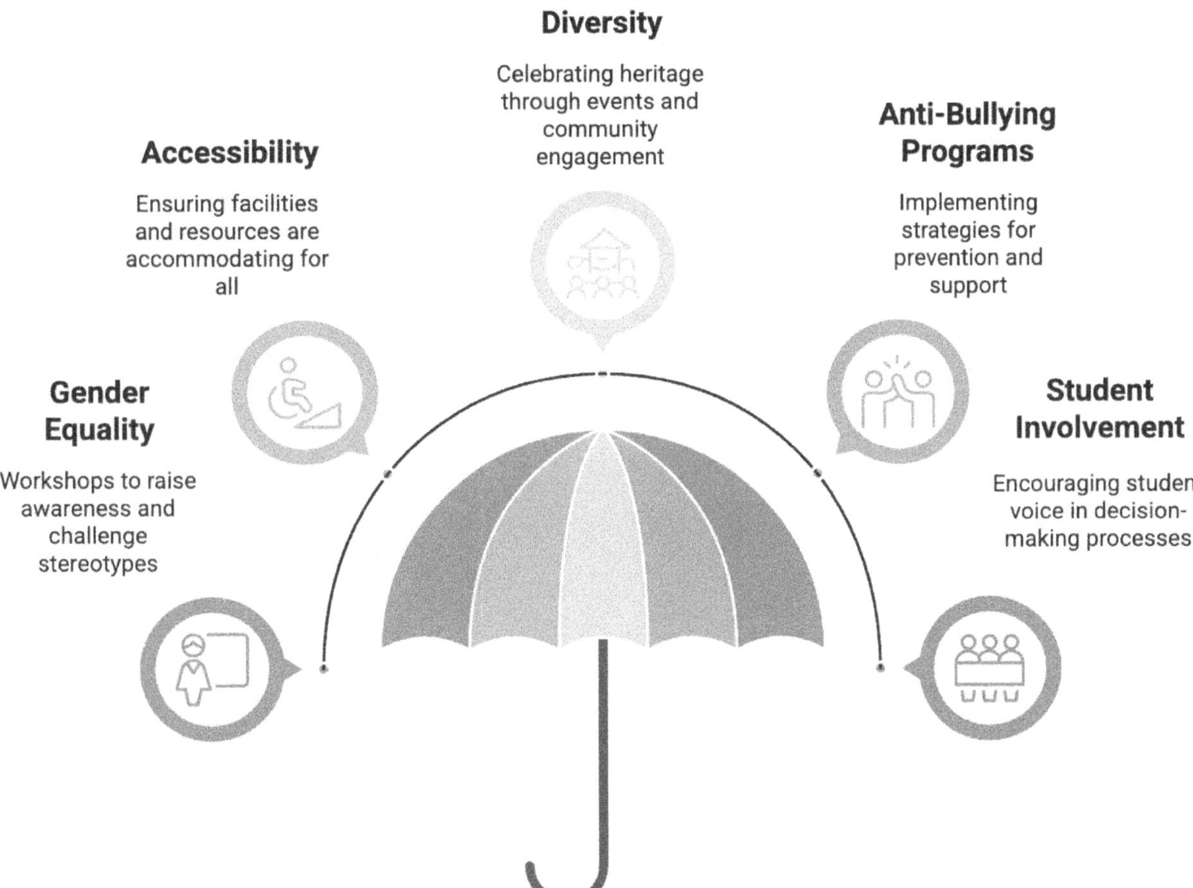

Building an Inclusive Education
Cultural Diversity
Celebrating heritage through events and community engagement
Accessibility
Ensuring facilities and resources are accommodating for all
Anti-Bullying Programs
Implementing strategies for prevention and support
Gender Equality
Workshops to raise awareness and challenge stereotypes
Student Involvement
Encouraging student voice in decision-making processes

7. Green Practices

Reduce single-use plastics.

Start carpool or bike-to-school programs.

Use eco-friendly supplies.

Encourage digital submissions to reduce paper waste.

Host workshops on sustainable fashion.

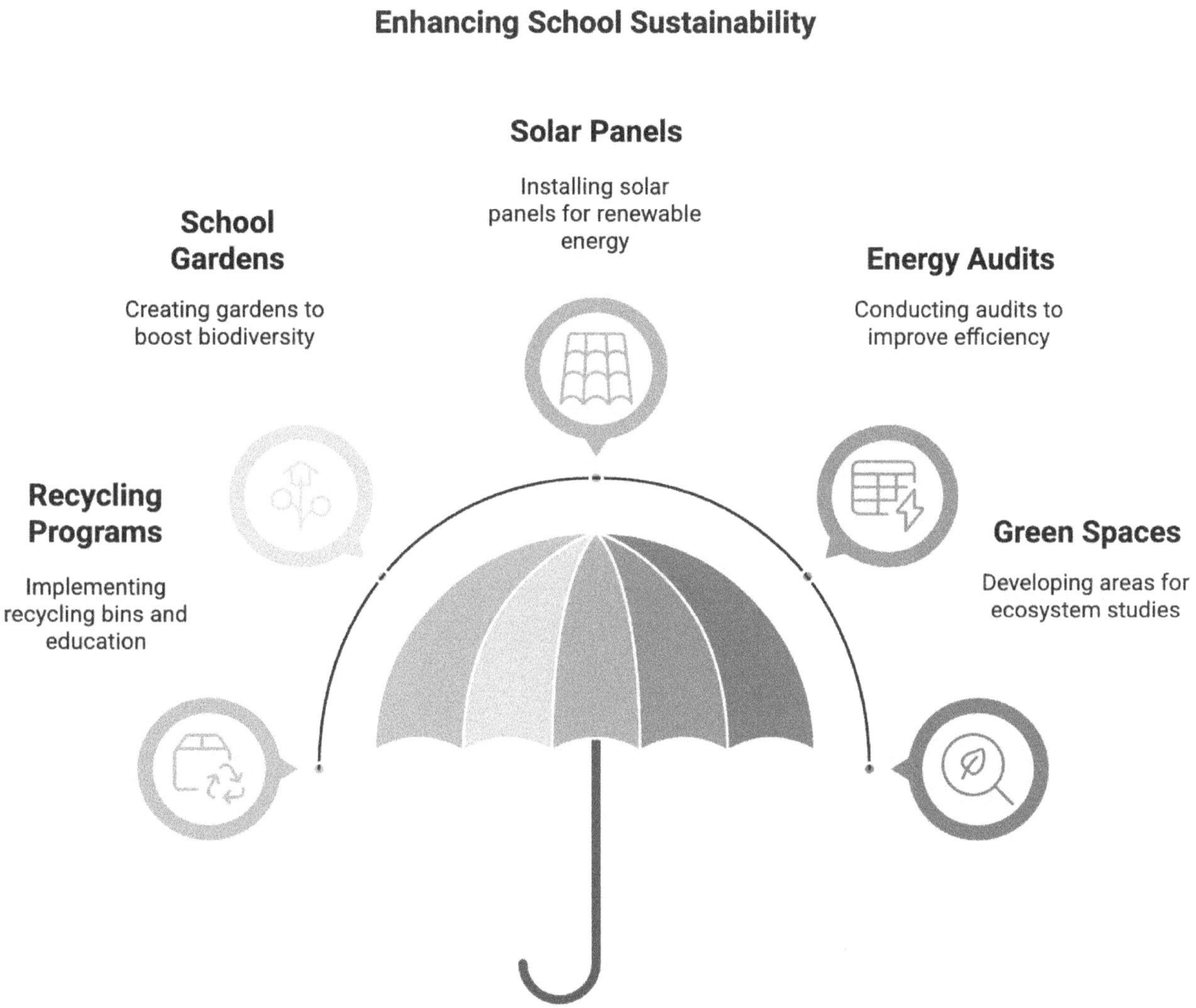

Enhancing School Sustainability

Solar Panels

Installing solar panels for renewable energy

School Gardens

Creating gardens to boost biodiversity

Energy Audits

Conducting audits to improve efficiency

Recycling Programs

Implementing recycling bins and education

Green Spaces

Developing areas for ecosystem studies

8. Global Citizenship

Teach local-global connections.

Include global perspectives in history and social studies.

Partner with international schools for cultural exchange.

Promote language learning for intercultural communication.

Support fair trade in school fundraising.

Strategies for Fostering Global Citizenship
Fair Trade Support
Promoting ethical consumerism and social responsibility
Local-Global Connections
Emphasizing the impact of local actions on global issues
Language Learning
Enhancing communication and cultural understanding
Global Perspectives
Incorporating diverse narratives in education
International Partnerships
Facilitating cultural exchange and collaboration

9. Technology and Innovation

Use tech for SDG research and presentations.

Share sustainability initiatives online.

Encourage coding and robotics projects for environmental solutions.

Provide online SDG learning resources.

Promote sustainability apps.

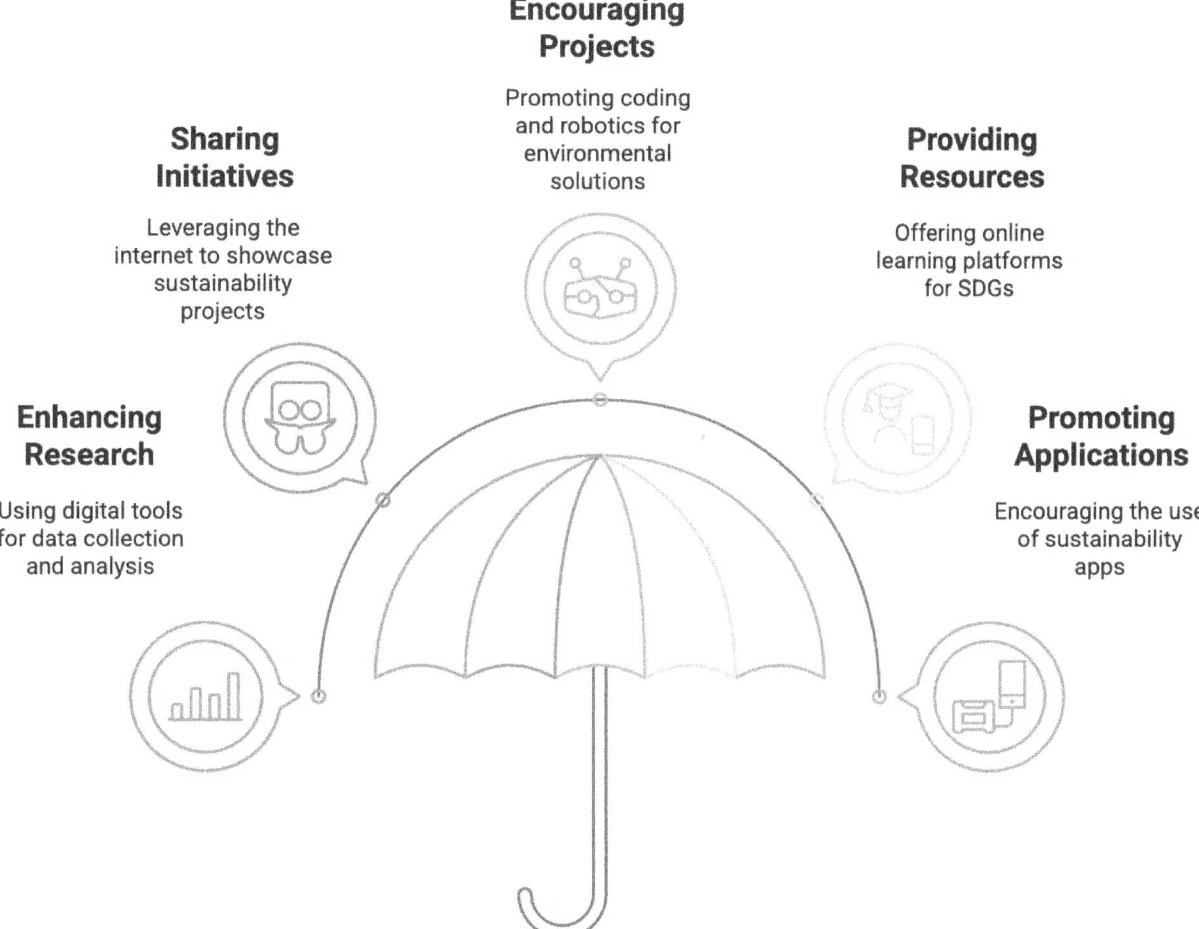

Technology's Role in Achieving SDGs
Encouraging Projects
Promoting coding and robotics for environmental solutions
Sharing Initiatives
Leveraging the internet to showcase sustainability projects
Providing Resources
Offering online learning platforms for SDGs
Enhancing Research
Using digital tools for data collection and analysis
Promoting Applications
Encouraging the use of sustainability apps

10. Monitoring and Evaluation

Set measurable sustainability goals.

Conduct student surveys on SDG awareness.

Report progress to the community.

Collect feedback from students and staff.

Celebrate SDG achievements.

Monitoring and Evaluating Sustainability Goals

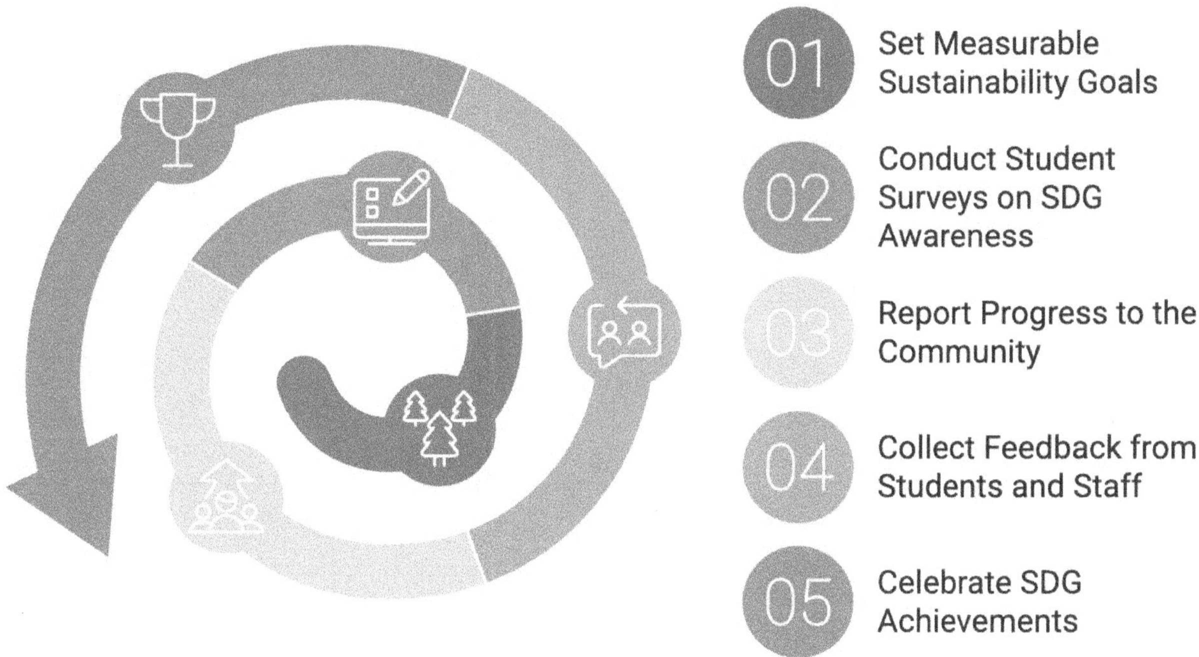

11. Teacher Training

Train teachers to integrate SDGs into lessons.

Encourage attendance at sustainability conferences.

Create professional learning communities.

Share best practices among educators.

Support interdisciplinary teacher collaboration.

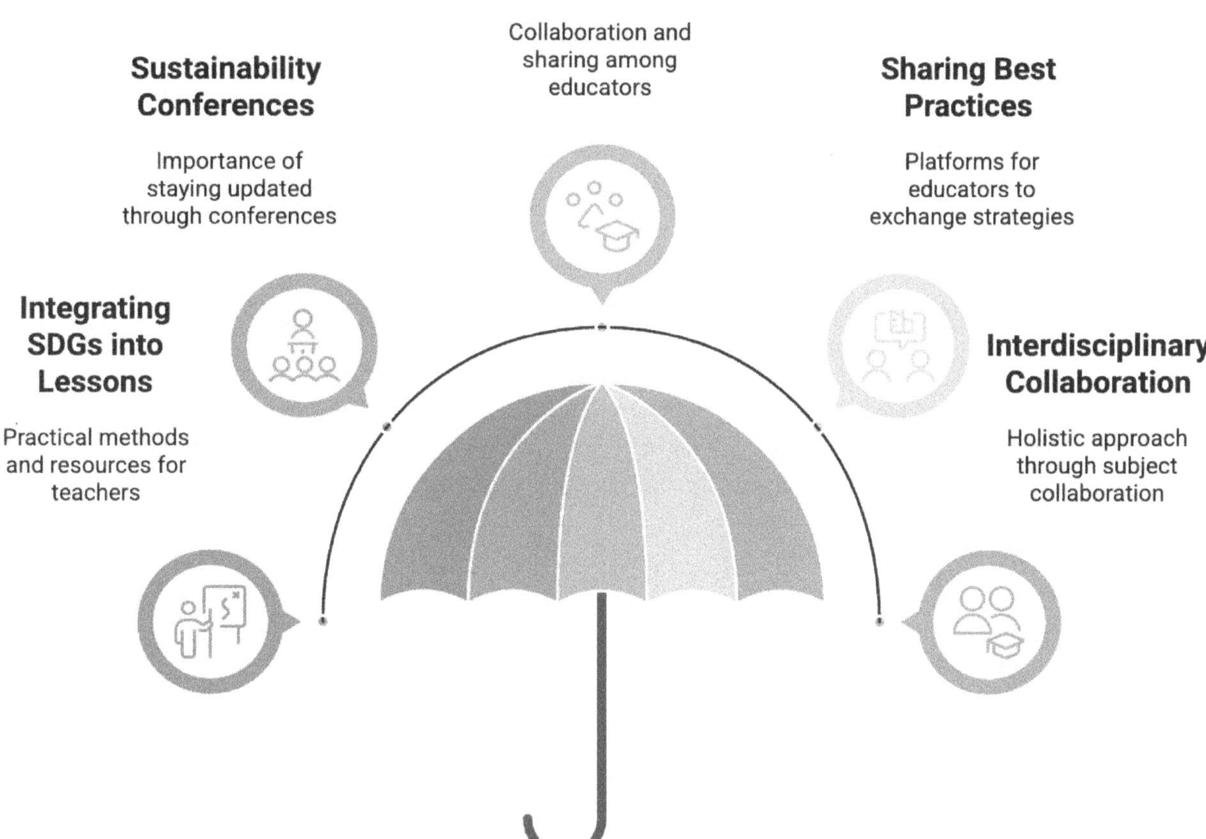
Strategies for Integrating SDGs in Education
Professional Learning Communities
Collaboration and sharing among educators
Sustainability Conferences
Importance of staying updated through conferences
Sharing Best Practices
Platforms for educators to exchange strategies
Integrating SDGs into Lessons
Practical methods and resources for teachers
Interdisciplinary Collaboration
Holistic approach through subject collaboration

12. Extracurricular Activities

Organize field trips to sustainable farms or NGOs.

Host SDG film screenings and discussions.

Promote environmental competitions.

Use art to raise sustainability awareness.

Create an SDG-focused school newspaper or blog.

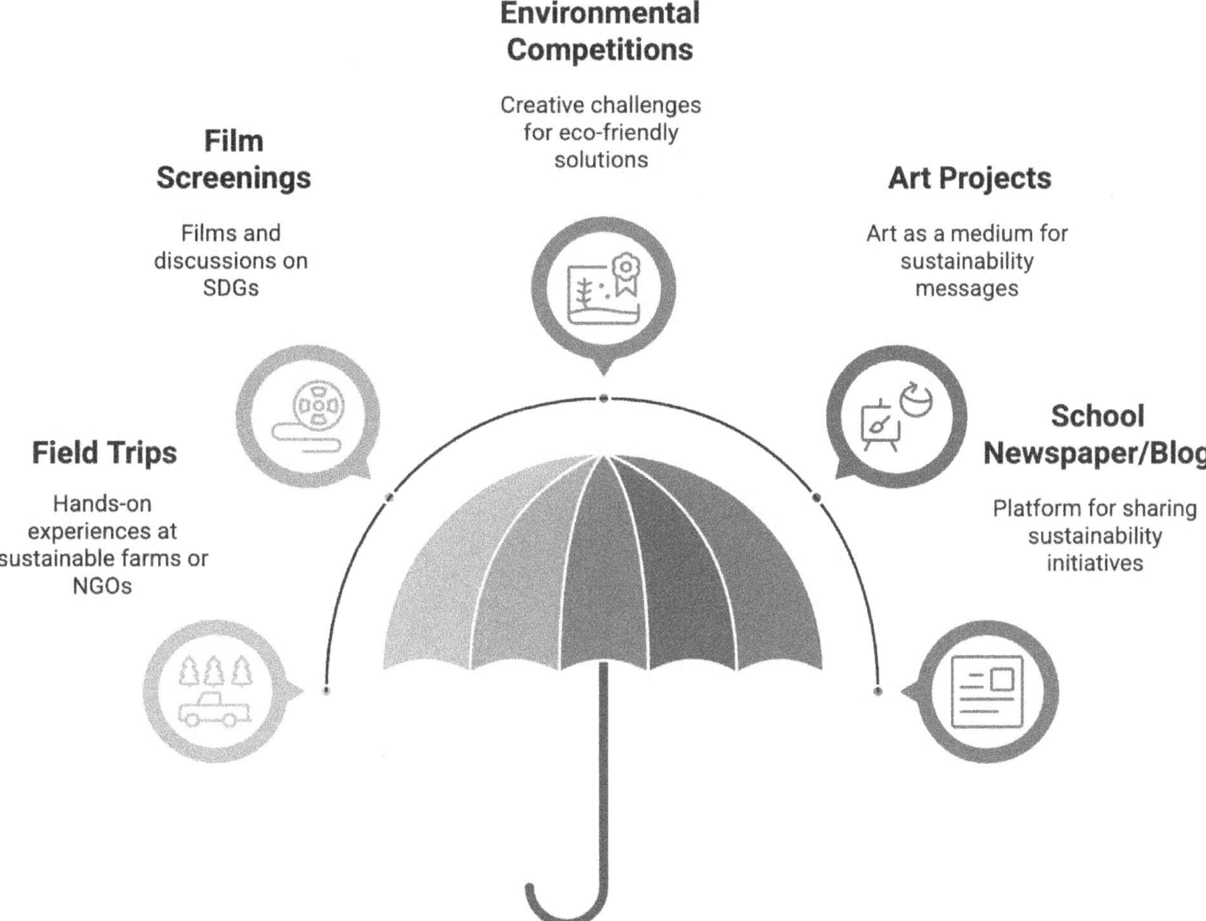

Engaging Students in Sustainability
Environmental Competitions
Creative challenges for eco-friendly solutions
Film Screenings
Films and discussions on SDGs
Art Projects
Art as a medium for sustainability messages
Field Trips
Hands-on experiences at sustainable farms or NGOs
School Newspaper/Blog
Platform for sharing sustainability initiatives

13. Partnerships

Collaborate with universities for research.

Partner with local businesses for sustainability projects.

Work with NGOs for educational activities.

Engage parents in sustainability discussions.

Build a school network for sharing SDG resources.

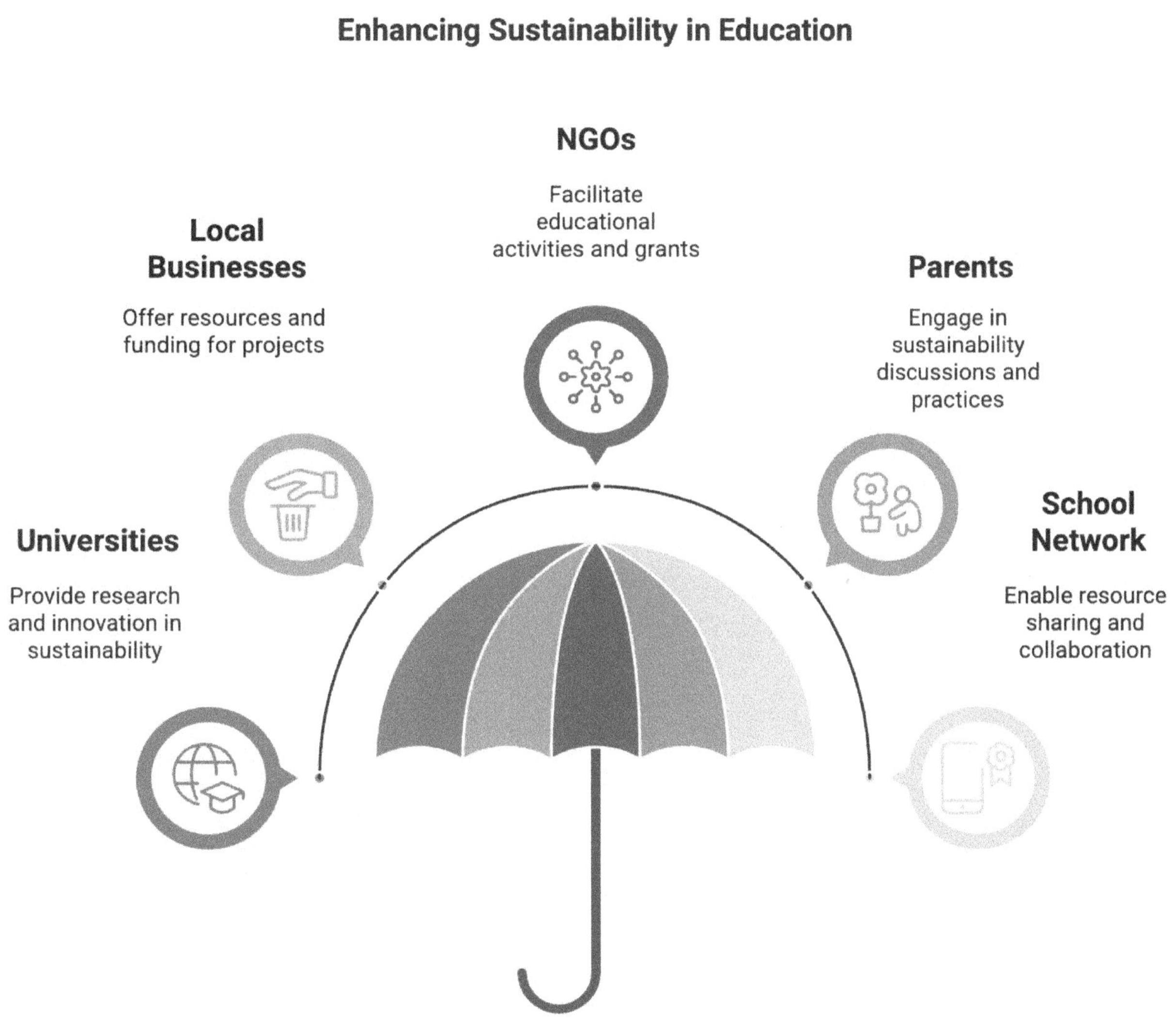

Enhancing Sustainability in Education
NGOs
Facilitate educational activities and grants
Local Businesses
Offer resources and funding for projects
Parents
Engage in sustainability discussions and practices
Universities
Provide research and innovation in sustainability
School Network
Enable resource sharing and collaboration

14. Advocacy and Awareness

Run SDG awareness campaigns.

Encourage students to write to local leaders.

Create posters and infographics.

Promote SDG initiatives on social media.

Celebrate "Sustainable Development Goals Day."

Strategies for SDG Advocacy

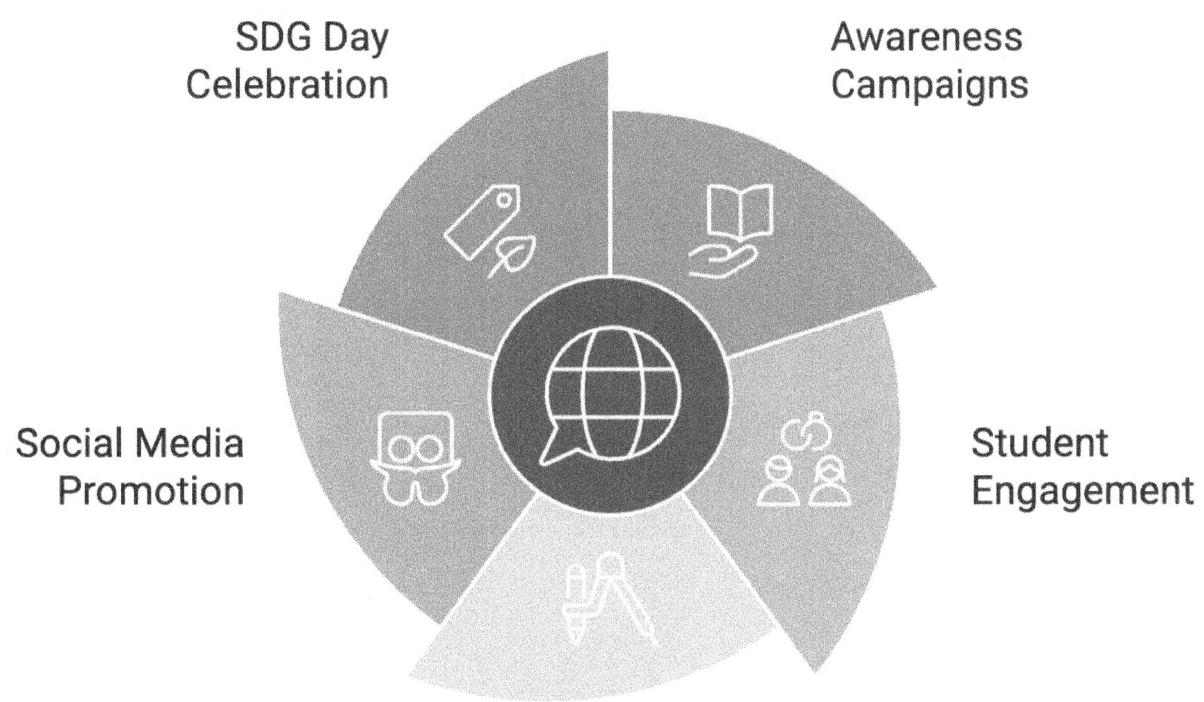

15. Financial Literacy

Teach sustainable finance and investment.

Include economic sustainability in lessons.

Encourage sustainable business plans.

Discuss the environmental impact of consumer choices.

Teach budgeting for sustainability.

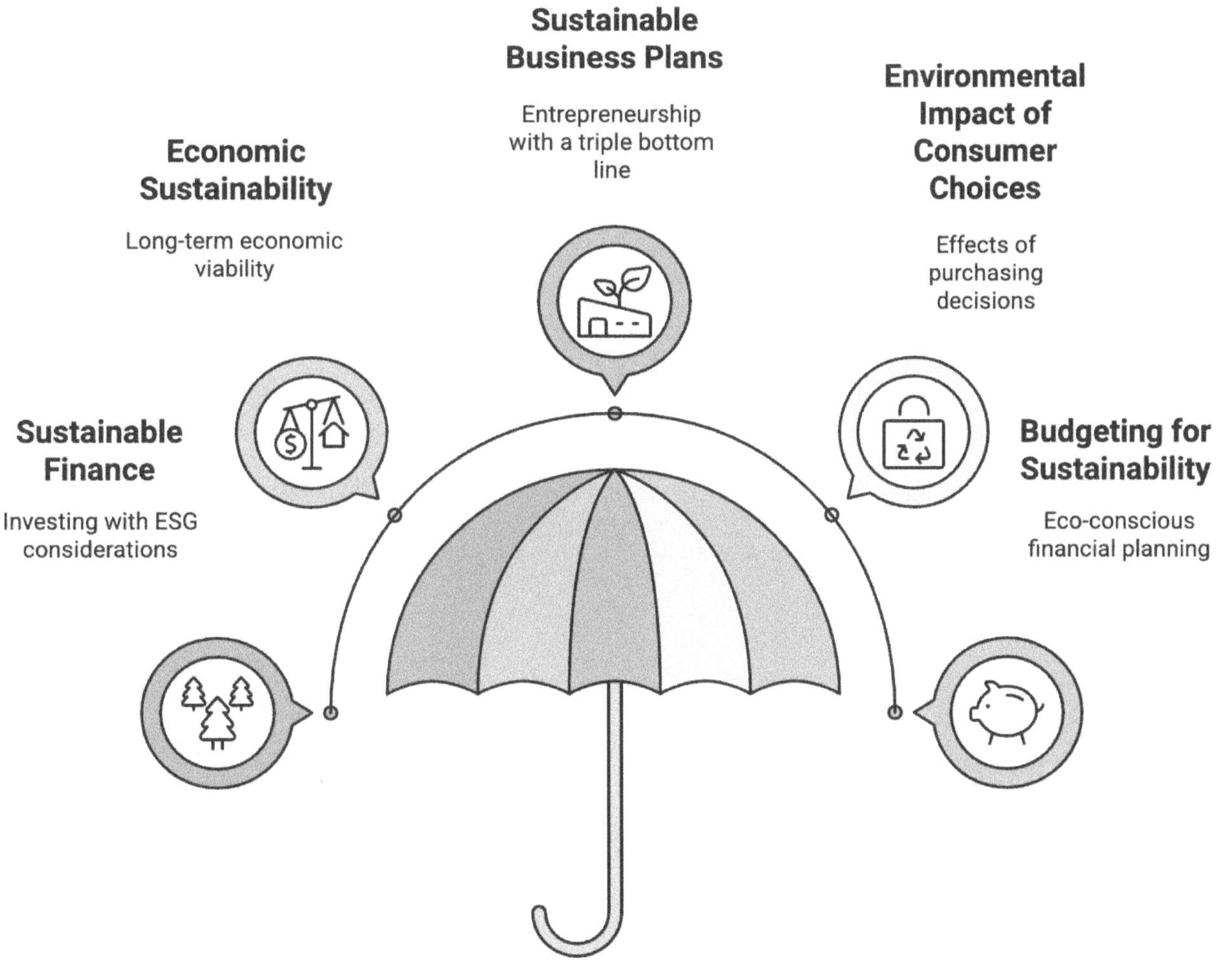
Pathways to Sustainable Financial Literacy
Sustainable Business Plans
Entrepreneurship with a triple bottom line
Environmental Impact of Consumer Choices
Effects of purchasing decisions
Economic Sustainability
Long-term economic viability
Budgeting for Sustainability
Eco-conscious financial planning
Sustainable Finance
Investing with ESG considerations

16. Research and Innovation

Encourage student research on local sustainability.

Host SDG innovation challenges.

Invite sustainability experts as mentors.

Organize science fairs focused on environmental and social innovation.

Integrate sustainability into STEM education.

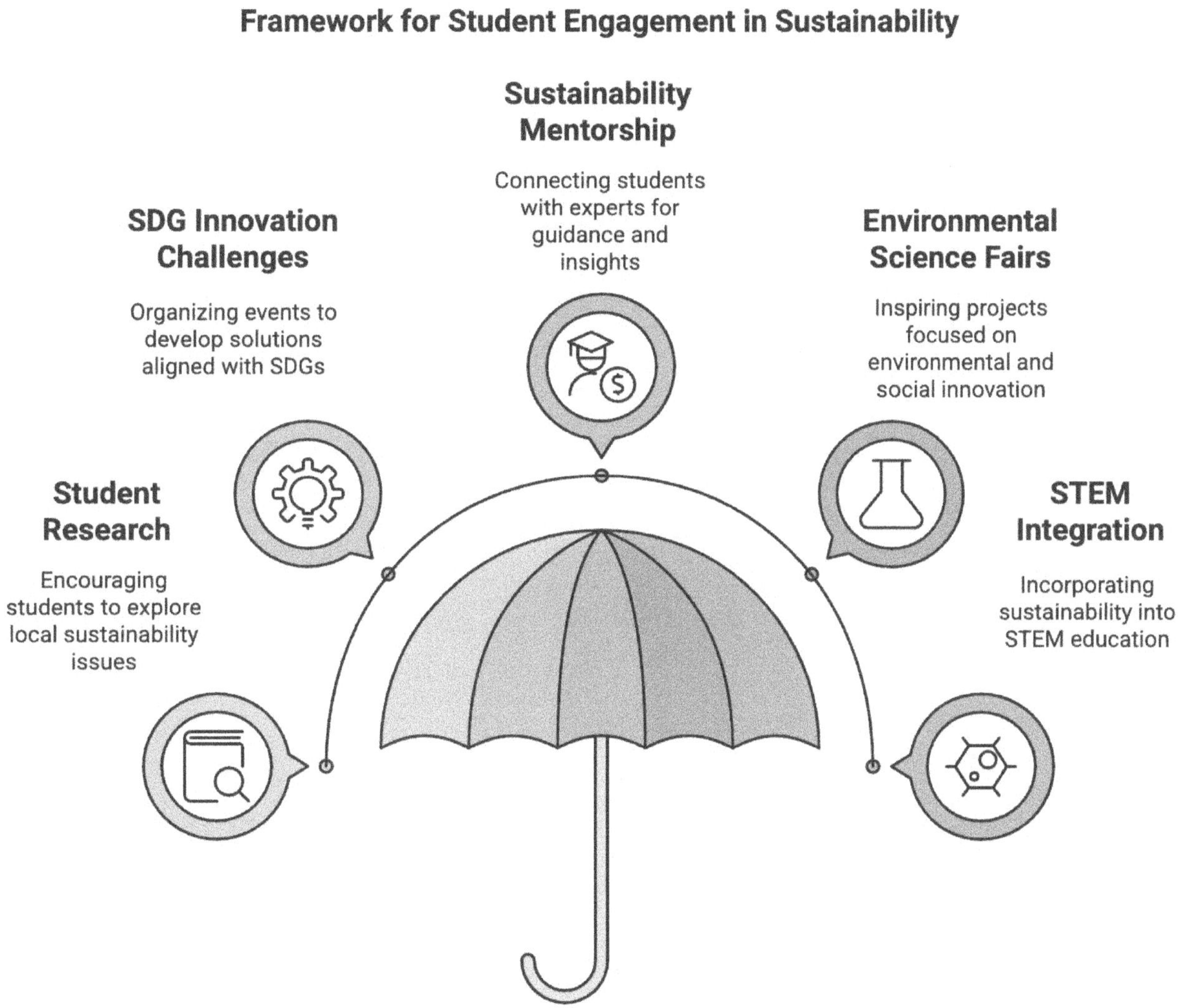

Framework for Student Engagement in Sustainability

Sustainability Mentorship

Connecting students with experts for guidance and insights

SDG Innovation Challenges

Organizing events to develop solutions aligned with SDGs

Environmental Science Fairs

Inspiring projects focused on environmental and social innovation

Student Research

Encouraging students to explore local sustainability issues

STEM Integration

Incorporating sustainability into STEM education

17. Celebrating Diversity

Share stories of sustainability practices from different cultures.

Please encourage students to share their cultural and environmental practices.

Celebrate global SDG days.

Create an inclusive environment for all voices.

Promote indigenous knowledge and traditions.

Global Sustainability Practices Overview

18. Long-Term Commitment

Develop a school sustainability policy.

Form a sustainability committee with students and staff.

Create a long-term SDG action plan.

Regularly review and update sustainability goals.

Involve alumni in sustainability efforts.

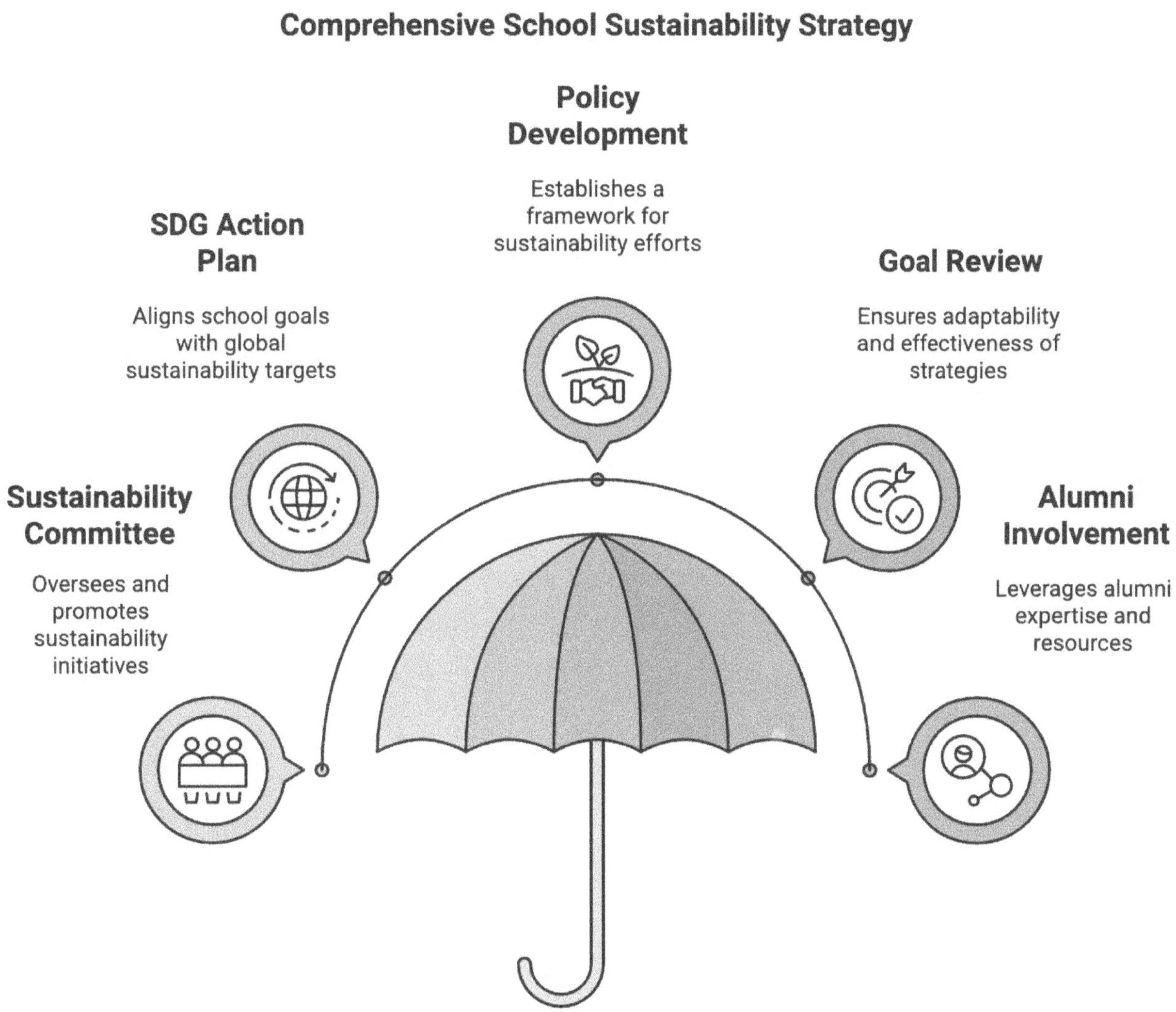
Comprehensive School Sustainability Strategy
Policy Development
Establishes a framework for sustainability efforts
SDG Action Plan
Aligns school goals with global sustainability targets
Goal Review
Ensures adaptability and effectiveness of strategies
Sustainability Committee
Oversees and promotes sustainability initiatives
Alumni Involvement
Leverages alumni expertise and resources

19. Celebrating Success

Recognize student and staff sustainability efforts.

Award outstanding sustainability projects.

Share success stories with the community.

Host an annual sustainability fair.

Highlight ongoing activities in newsletters.

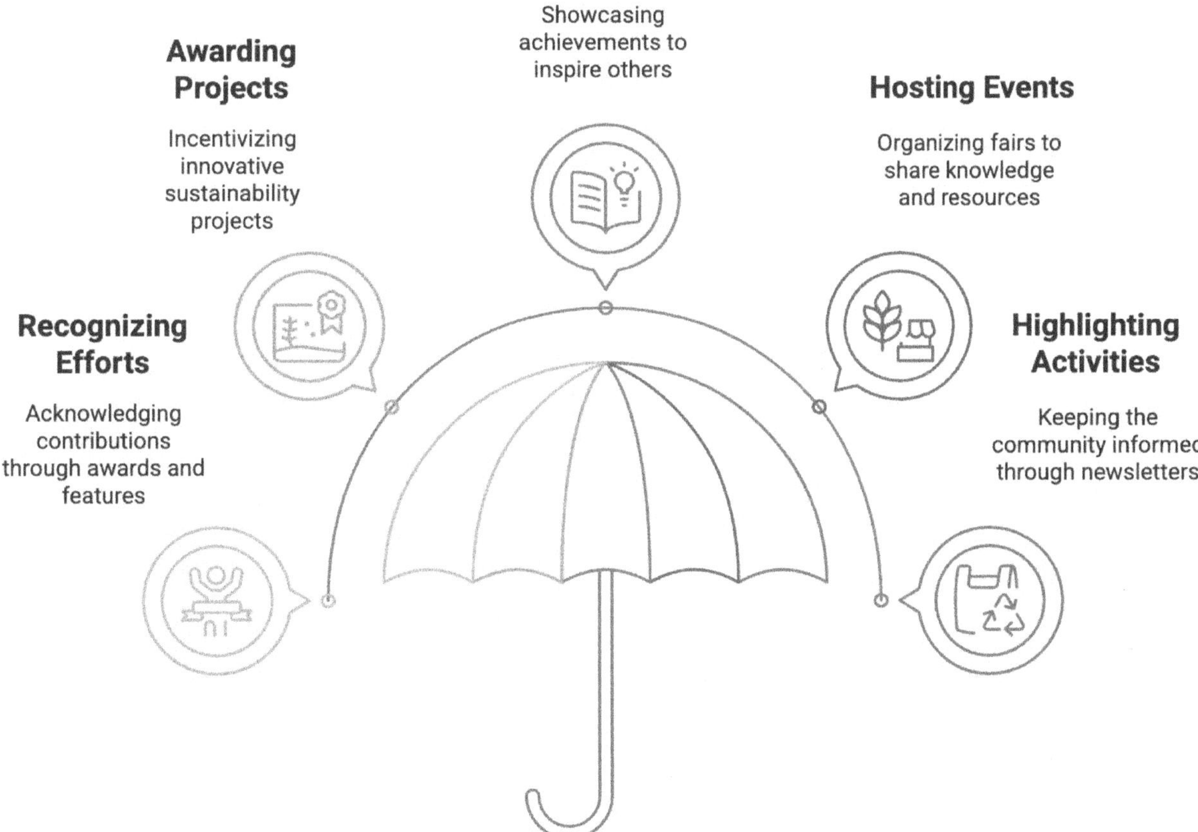
Celebrating Sustainability Success
Sharing
Success
Stories
Showcasing achievements to inspire others
Awarding Projects
Incentivizing innovative sustainability projects
Hosting Events
Organizing fairs to share knowledge and resources
Recognizing Efforts
Acknowledging contributions through awards and features
Highlighting Activities
Keeping the community informed through newsletters

20. Lifelong Learning

Stay updated on global sustainability trends.

Encourage students to pursue sustainability studies.

Provide lifelong SDG learning resources.

Foster a culture of curiosity about sustainability.

Continuously improve sustainability practices.

Pathways to Sustainability

CHAPTER NINE

ABOUT THE AUTHOR

Dr. Dheeraj Mehrotra, is a distinguished educational leader and innovator with over three decades of experience transforming education through excellence and innovation. A recipient of the President of India's National Teacher Award (2006), he is a certified expert in Six Sigma (White and Yellow Belt), Neuro-Linguistic Programming (NLP), and Total Quality Management (TQM). His specialisation encompasses academic audits, school quality assurance and accreditation (SQAA), and implementing Kaizen and 5S in schools. As an accomplished author, Dr. Mehrotra has published over 200 books on various subjects, including computer science, artificial intelligence, digital body language, quality circles, and school management. His contributions also include the development of more than 150 free educational mobile apps for teachers, students, and parents, a feat recognised by the Limca Book of Records and the India Book of Records. Dr. Mehrotra has served as Principal at prestigious institutions such as De Indian Public School in New Delhi, NPS International School in Guwahati, and Kunwar's Global School in Lucknow. He has also held the position of Education Officer at GEMS in Gurgaon, making significant contributions to the global education community. As a premier UDEMY instructor, Dr. Mehrotra has created over 500 courses that have impacted more than 800,000 learners across 180 countries. Additionally, as the founder and president of the IoT Society of India, he advocates for technology integration in education worldwide.

www.authordheerajmehrotra.com

BOOKS BY THE SAME AUTHOR

www.authordheerajmehrotra.com